WASHINGTON, D.C.

# 1,000 FACTS ABOUT THE WHITE HOUSE

SARAH WASSNER FLYNN    FOREWORD BY STEWART D. McLAURIN

NATIONAL GEOGRAPHIC

WASHINGTON, D.C.

# TABLE OF CONTENTS

## 1,000 FACTS ABOUT THE WHITE HOUSE

North Portico and lawn
of the White House

# FOREWORD

Learning about the White House inevitably begins by asking two questions: "Who lives there?" and "Why is it white?" But for some, these questions may be just the beginning of a career devoted to studying, preserving, or teaching the history of the President's House and those who lived there.

As you will discover, the lively 1,000 fun facts presented so colorfully on the following pages are simply an introduction to the continually unfolding story of American history centered in the most famous house in the nation, an icon of its history and an emblem of American democracy. As you learn about the first, last, only, most, least, biggest, and smallest features and events associated with this national treasure at 1600 Pennsylvania Avenue, consider studying more about the topics that interest you most. There will always be new chapters to be written and more history to uncover.

The White House Historical Association and publishers like National Geographic share a devotion to bringing history to life. We invite you to learn more from our books and online resources as you investigate subjects related to White House history such as the presidents and the first families, architecture, gardens, fine art, fashion, technology, and travel. I hope this introduction to the President's House will inspire you to ask questions, pursue answers, and join us on a never ending adventure in learning.

STEWART D. McLAURIN
President, White House Historical Association

# 10 FAST FACTS
## YOU NEED TO KNOW ABOUT

**1**
LOCATED AT 1600 PENNSYLVANIA AVENUE IN WASHINGTON, D.C., THE WHITE HOUSE SERVES AS THE **HOME** AND **OFFICE** OF **THE PRESIDENT OF THE UNITED STATES.**

**3**
JOHN ADAMS, the second U.S. president, was the **FIRST TO LIVE** in the White House.

**5**
When open for tours, the White House can recieve as many as about **6,000** VISITORS.

**6**
THE WHITE HOUSE IS **ONE OF THE FEW** PRIVATE RESIDENCES OF HEADS OF STATE WORLDWIDE THAT IS **OPEN TO THE PUBLIC FREE OF CHARGE.**

**2**
SINCE IT WAS BUILT IN 1800, **43 PRESIDENTS** HAVE LIVED IN THE WHITE HOUSE.

**4**
The White House was once the **LARGEST HOME** in the United States.

# THE WHITE HOUSE

**7**

The 18 acres (7.3 ha) enclosed by the White House **FENCE** are set within the surrounding 85-acre (34.4-ha) area known as **PRESIDENT'S PARK.**

**8**

The White House complex includes the **EXECUTIVE RESIDENCE, WEST WING, EAST WING, EISENHOWER EXECUTIVE OFFICE BUILDING,** and **BLAIR HOUSE,** a guest residence.

**9**

THE WHITE HOUSE IS FEATURED ON THE BACK OF THE **U.S. $20 BILL.**

**10**

President **Theodore Roosevelt** officially named the building the White House in 1901. Until then, it was known as the **PRESIDENT'S HOUSE** or the **EXECUTIVE MANSION.**

# THE WHITE HOUSE

Welcome to President's Park, enclosing the White House buildings. The park lies at the heart of Washington, D.C. It includes lawns with fountains, statues, and monuments; gardens; a tennis court and swimming pool; and is crossed by two main thoroughfares— Pennsylvania Avenue and E Street Northwest.

## West Wing
the White House addition housing the Oval Office, the Cabinet Room, the Situation Room, the Roosevelt Room, the Press Briefing Room, and offices for the president's closest aides

## Eisenhower Building
houses offices for the White House staff; once used by the State, War, and Navy Departments

## South Lawn
the president's backyard, where the Easter Egg Roll takes place and Marine One helicopters land and take off

## National Christmas Tree
large Christmas tree that the president lights, a tradition started in 1923

## Ellipse
a lawn to the south of the White House where events are often held; it is open to the public

# BUILDINGS AND GARDENS

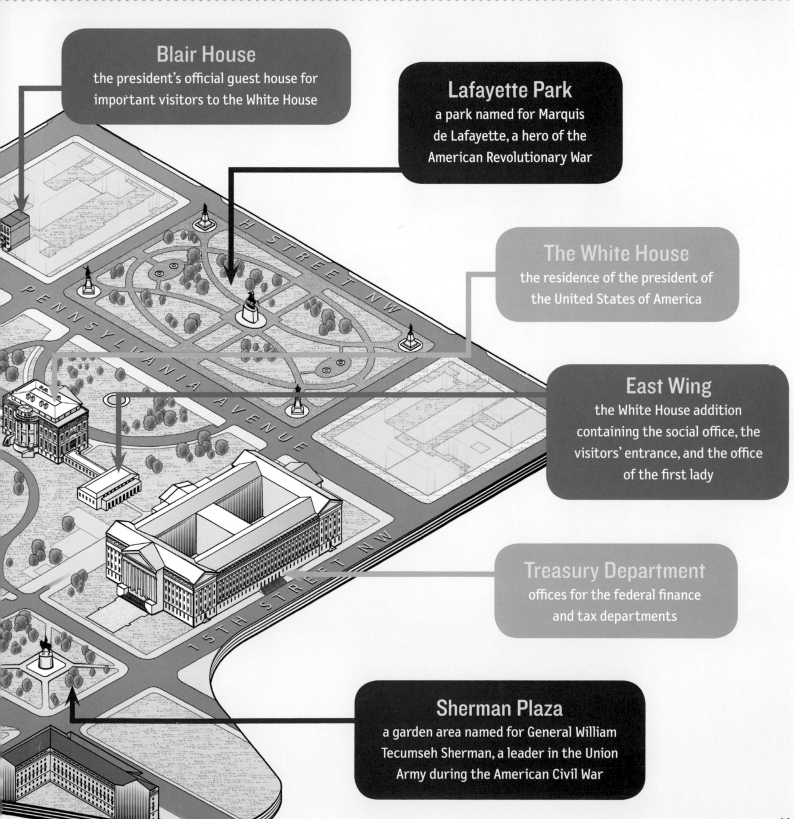

**Blair House**
the president's official guest house for important visitors to the White House

**Lafayette Park**
a park named for Marquis de Lafayette, a hero of the American Revolutionary War

**The White House**
the residence of the president of the United States of America

**East Wing**
the White House addition containing the social office, the visitors' entrance, and the office of the first lady

**Treasury Department**
offices for the federal finance and tax departments

**Sherman Plaza**
a garden area named for General William Tecumseh Sherman, a leader in the Union Army during the American Civil War

H STREET NW

PENNSYLVANIA AVENUE

15TH STREET NW

**1**

There are **132 ROOMS** and **6 LEVELS** in the White House Residence.

**2**

The White House's **RED**, **GREEN**, and **BLUE** rooms are all named for the color of the **CARPET**, **WALLS**, and **FABRICS** in each room.

**3**

Mary Abigail Fillmore, daughter of President Millard Fillmore, *played her harp* for guests in the *Yellow Oval Room*, which is still used as a living room.

**4**

ABRAHAM LINCOLN *never slept in the* LINCOLN BEDROOM—*it was his personal office where he signed the* EMANCIPATION PROCLAMATION. *Some of his furniture remains there today.*

**5**

THE Queens' Bedroom, ON THE SECOND FLOOR OF THE WHITE HOUSE RESIDENCE, IS NAMED FOR THE VARIOUS **royal guests** WHO HAVE STAYED THERE.

# 25 FACTS ABOUT ROOMS

**6**

British prime minister **WINSTON CHURCHILL** stayed in the **QUEENS' BEDROOM** when he visited with presidents Franklin D. Roosevelt and Harry S. Truman.

**7**

DURING THE EARLY 1800s, IT'S SAID THAT FIRST LADY ABIGAIL ADAMS WOULD hang her laundry IN THE East Room OF THE WHITE HOUSE.

**8**

Today, the **EAST ROOM**, the **LARGEST** room in the White House, is used for **SPECIAL EVENTS**, like concerts.

**12**

Created during World War II, the **MAP ROOM** houses **WORLD MAPS** produced by National Geographic.

**9**

A **PIANO** IN THE EAST ROOM WITH LEGS CARVED INTO THE SHAPE OF **AMERICAN EAGLES** WAS GIVEN TO PRESIDENT FRANKLIN D. ROOSEVELT SOME **80 YEARS AGO.**

**10**

First Lady **MICHELLE OBAMA** once challenged talk show host Jimmy Fallon to a **POTATO SACK RACE** in the East Room.

**11**

President Barack Obama met with the **DALAI LAMA** in the Map Room.

**13** The historic **WALLPAPER** in the Diplomatic Reception Room was selected by First Lady Jacqueline Kennedy in **1962.**

**14** THE WHITE HOUSE THEATER IS A SPOT FOR THE FIRST FAMILY AND THEIR GUESTS TO WATCH MOVIES, SPORTS, AND THEIR FAVORITE TV SHOWS.

**15** The theater seats 42 people and includes large, **COMFY ARMCHAIRS** for the president and first family.

**16** THERE ARE 240-YEAR-OLD CHAIRS IN THE WHITE HOUSE COLLECTION ONCE USED BY PRESIDENT GEORGE WASHINGTON IN HIS HOMES IN NEW YORK AND PHILADELPHIA.

**17** Today's **CHINA ROOM** was designated by **FIRST LADY EDITH WILSON** in 1917 to display examples of dishes used by nearly every **PRESIDENT.**

# THAT ROCK

**18** President Rutherford B. Hayes took the **OATH OF OFFICE** in the Red Room.

**19** THE **BLUE ROOM** WAS NOT ALWAYS BLUE—IT WAS RED UNTIL PRESIDENT MARTIN VAN BUREN CHANGED THE **COLOR SCHEME** IN **1837.**

**20** The **OVAL SHAPE** of the **BLUE ROOM** was inspired by President Washington. He had a similar-shaped room in his presidential home in **PHILADELPHIA.**

**25** First Lady **ABIGAIL FILLMORE** helped build the **WHITE HOUSE LIBRARY** and also made sure the home had a **MUSIC ROOM.**

**21** During President Ulysses S. Grant's administration, the RED ROOM was used as a family **LIVING ROOM.**

**22** The **White House** collection of vermeil—silver objects dipped in gold—is showcased in cabinets in the **VERMEIL,** or **GOLD,** Room.

**23** There are more than 1,000 **PIECES** of **VERMEIL** in the collection, dating back to the **18TH CENTURY.**

**24** UNTIL PRESIDENT MILLARD FILLMORE BUILT ITS FIRST LIBRARY IN THE EARLY 1850s, THERE WAS NO PERMANENT COLLECTION OF BOOKS IN THE WHITE HOUSE.

**1**
The West Wing—the White House's **center of official presidential business**—contains the **Oval Office** and the Cabinet, Situation, Roosevelt, and Press Briefing Rooms.

**2**
During the first 100 years of the White House, the building did not have an **Oval Office.**

**3**
Before the **West Wing** was built in 1902, presidential staff usually worked on the second floor of what is now the Executive Residence.

**4**
President Theodore Roosevelt had the **West Wing** built on the site of a **greenhouse** and **stables.**

**5**
There are several offices for the president's staff in the **West Wing,** ranging from tiny cubicles to large spaces with windows—and a **view.**

**6**
President Theodore Roosevelt's office was **rectangular,** not oval. That same room is now known as the **Roosevelt Room** and functions as a conference room.

**7**
President Franklin D. Roosevelt kept an **aquarium** and **mounted fish** he'd caught on the walls of the room, so it was temporarily named the **Fish Room.**

**8**
In 1909, President William Howard Taft added the Oval Office, forever connecting the **residential** and **official business** areas.

**9**
President Taft held a **contest** to find an **architect** to **design** an executive work space.

**10**
Nathan C. Wyeth, an **architect** from Washington, D.C., won with the **oval-shape design.**

**11**
President Herbert Hoover brought the **first telephone** into the **Oval Office** in 1929.

**12**
A **Christmas Eve** fire in 1929 **gutted** the White House's West Wing.

**13**
During the 1929 **fire,** President Hoover had to leave his Christmas party to oversee the removal of some **200,000 important papers** from the Oval Office.

**14**
President Hoover moved back into the **rebuilt West Wing** less than **four months** after the fire.

**15**
President Franklin D. Roosevelt later **moved the Oval Office** to its present spot in the southeast corner of the West Wing and **added windows.**

**16**
During World War II, **windows** behind the president's desk in the Oval Office were fitted with **bulletproof glass.**

**17**
Nineteen U.S. presidents have **conducted business** in the **Oval Office** since it was first constructed in 1909.

**18**
Today, the Oval Office is considered to be the **most famous and iconic office** in the world.

**19**
There's a **replica** of the Oval Office at the **LBJ Presidential Library** in Austin, Texas.

**20**
The desk used by many recent presidents in the Oval Office—the **Resolute desk**—was a gift from England's **Queen Victoria.**

**21**
The **Resolute desk** got its name because it was built with reclaimed wood from a **British ship** called the H.M.S. *Resolute.*

**22**
President **Barack Obama** was repeatedly photographed **resting his feet** on the famous desk.

**23**
President Franklin D. Roosevelt, who suffered from polio, added a front panel to the Resolute desk to **hide** the **braces on his legs.**

**24**
Before moving out of the Oval Office, President Ronald Reagan **left a note** for President George H. W. Bush in one of the **desk's drawers.**

**25**
Presidents Reagan and Bill Clinton both displayed a **wooden sign** on their executive desks saying "It can be done."

**26**
President **John F. Kennedy** installed a **secret taping system** in the Oval Office, probably to help him write his memoir.

**27**
President Franklin D. Roosevelt also secretly recorded Oval Office meetings through a **microphone** hidden in his **desk lamp.**

**28**
President Richard M. Nixon had a secret taping system installed that **turned on** and **off automatically** as people spoke then went silent—it was "voice activated."

**29**
The Oval Office contains **four doors** connecting it to the Rose Garden, a private dining room, a hallway, and the president's secretary's office.

**30**
There are two "secret" doors in the Oval Office, designed to **blend** into the **walls.**

**31**
The president often eats in the **Navy Mess**, a **dining room** on the ground floor of the West Wing run by the U.S. Navy.

**32**
The Navy Mess was **established** by President Harry S. Truman in 1951.

**33**
"Mess hall" is a **military term** for **dining area** or **cafeteria**.

**34**
President Lyndon B. Johnson's Oval Office desk chair was a **green vinyl helicopter seat**—a nod to his love of choppers.

**35**
The president holds **regular meetings** with his Cabinet secretaries and other administration officials in the **Cabinet Room.**

**36**
The color of the first carpet in the **Oval Office** was **green.** In recent years, each president has chosen a unique design.

**37**
In 1970, President Nixon spent **$4,000** of his personal funds to buy the 20-seat **mahogany table** still used in the **Cabinet Room** today.

**38**
The **Situation Room**—a complex of rooms on the West Wing's ground floor—is also known as the **woodshed.**

**39**
U.S. presidents have been using the **Situation Room** for intelligence and information gathering for more than **50 years.**

**40**
In this room, the staff **briefs the president** on important issues so he can make a **decision** on the "situation."

**41**
The president speaks to **foreign leaders** via **videoconference** from the Situation Room.

**42**
At the flick of a switch, **windows** in the Situation Room **frost over** to give the president **privacy.**

**43**
The Situation Room is staffed by **military aides** 24 hours a day, seven days a week.

**44**
The **phone booth** in the Situation Room is known as the **Superman tube** because it looks similar to the one the action hero uses in comic books.

**45**
No unauthorized texting or **cell phone calls** are allowed in the Situation Room.

**46**
Four **marines**—trained to stand perfectly still—are always **on guard** at the West Wing of the White House when the president is in the Oval Office.

**47**
The James S. Brady Press Briefing Room was a **laundry room**, then an indoor **swimming pool**, before it was turned into a spot for daily reports.

**48**
The **empty indoor pool** is still beneath the floor of the briefing room and can be accessed by a **trap door.**

**49**
The room is named for **James Brady**, the White House press secretary who was shot during the 1981 **assassination attempt** on President Ronald Reagan.

**50**
When speaking in the briefing room, the president stands behind two specially designed **bulletproof lecterns** known as **blue goose** and **blue falcon.**

# 50
## Facts About the
# WEST WING

❶ Some **100 people** work full-time in the **White House Residence.**

❷ White House Residence job openings are sometimes filled by **word of mouth** and by recommendations from current employees.

❸ White House Residence jobs include **ushers, florists,** curators, housekeepers, executive chefs, plumbers, **carpenters, police,** and window cleaners.

❹ President Martin Van Buren hired a full-time, **live-in fireman** to stoke the **White House's** massive furnace.

❺ There's a fully functioning **dentist and doctor's office** in the White House basement.

❻ As one president's family moves out, a **cleaning staff** of 95 has just five hours to **tidy up** the White House before the **arrival** of the next president's family.

❼ During the **transition between presidents,** the private quarters and Oval Office are **redecorated** from furniture to flower arrangements to new **family photos** on the walls.

# WHITE HOUSE JOBS

**8** A **fire truck** and **crew** are always on hand anytime a **helicopter** takes off or lands at the White House.

**9** The presidential family has staffers to run errands and grocery shop, but the family is **billed monthly** for expenses like food and other personal items.

**10** President Franklin D. Roosevelt's assistant, known as Mac, helped him **bathe and dress.**

**11** Before all the White House was equipped with **running water,** live-in staffers had to **haul water** up from pumps and **bathe** in **tin tubs.**

**12** It took at least **10 gardeners** and volunteers to maintain First Lady Michelle Obama's White House **vegetable garden** on the South Lawn.

**13 National park rangers** work full-time to maintain the grounds surrounding the White House.

**14** The White House has employed a crew of **calligraphers**—who pen everything from **dinner invitations** to **menus**—since 1801.

**15** During the holiday season, White House calligraphers may address some **10,000** envelopes by hand.

**Fifth graders work with White House chefs to harvest vegetables from First Lady Michelle Obama's kitchen garden.**

**1** The president has hosted **OFFICIAL DINNERS** at the White House since the beginning of its history.

**2** THE DINNERS **HONORING** CONGRESS, THE PRESIDENT'S CABINET, OR OTHER DIGNITARIES USED TO BE CALLED **STATE DINNERS.**

**3** Today, the term "state dinner" refers to an official dinner hosted by the president to **HONOR A FOREIGN HEAD OF STATE.**

**4** IN 1871, PRESIDENT ULYSSES S. GRANT AND HIS WIFE HOSTED THE **FIRST EVER** STATE DINNER, WELCOMING KING DAVID KALĀKAUA OF THE SANDWICH ISLANDS, MODERN-DAY **HAWAII.**

**5** The **36 GUESTS** who attended the 1871 dinner enjoyed a **29-COURSE MEAL of FRENCH CUISINE.**

# 25 FACTS TO CHEW ON ABOUT WHITE HOUSE

**6** Originally, state dinner guests sat at **long banquet tables** in a formal setting.

**7** IN THE 1960s, FIRST LADY JACQUELINE KENNEDY BEGAN USING **CIRCULAR TABLES** TO SEAT MORE PEOPLE.

**8** The **STATE DINING ROOM,** named by President Andrew Jackson, can seat **120 PEOPLE** and is usually where state dinners are held.

**9** A blessing given by President **JOHN ADAMS** in **1800** is carved in the large **STONE MANTELPIECE** in the State Dining Room.

**10** Larger dinners are sometimes held in the **EAST ROOM** or in a **TENT** on the White House **SOUTH LAWN.**

**11** When the White House was being **renovated** during the Harry S. Truman administration from 1948 to 1952, state dinners were held in **local hotels.**

**12** In 1961, the Kennedys hosted a state dinner at **MOUNT VERNON**—George Washington's former home—with guests **ARRIVING BY BOAT.**

I Pray Heaven To Bestow THE BEST OF BLESSINGS ON This House
And All that shall hereafter Inhabit it. May none but Honest and Wise Men ever rule under This Roof.

**13**

THE STATE DINNER DRESS CODE IS ALWAYS **FANCY,** WITH MEN WEARING **TUXEDOS,** AND **BALL GOWNS** FOR THE WOMEN.

**14**

The MARINE BAND, which often plays at state dinners, has performed at White House events since 1801.

**15**

Other state dinner entertainment has included **BROADWAY** performers and **FAMOUS SINGERS** like Beyoncé.

**16**

For a 2015 state dinner in honor of the prime minister of **JAPAN,** the White House **WINDOWS** were decorated with **CRYSTAL CURTAINS.**

**17**

PREPARATIONS FOR STATE DINNERS— MENU PLANNING, DECOR, AND GUEST LISTS—CAN TAKE UP TO SIX MONTHS.

# STATE DINNERS

**18**

A White House **CHEF** once described the lavish state dinners as "bigger than the **BIGGEST WEDDINGS."**

**19**

AT A 2012 STATE DINNER FOR THE **BRITISH** PRIME MINISTER, GUESTS MUNCHED ON BISON WELLINGTON— **BUFFALO MEAT** WRAPPED IN **PUFF PASTRY.**

**20**

President Lyndon B. Johnson hosted a record-setting **54** state dinners in **FIVE YEARS.** George W. Bush hosted just six during his two terms.

**21**

*State dinners* **COST** *around* **$500,000** *on average.*

**22**

CELEBRITY CHEF MARIO BATALI PREPARED PASTA FOR **500 GUESTS** AT PRESIDENT BARACK OBAMA'S 2016 STATE DINNER HONORING **ITALY'S PRIME MINISTER** MATTEO RENZI AND HIS WIFE.

**23**

AT STATE DINNERS, A **HANDWRITTEN MENU,** WHICH GUESTS CAN TAKE HOME AS A **SOUVENIR,** IS PLACED ON EVERY PLATE.

**24**

THE **UNITED KINGDOM** HAS BEEN HONORED WITH THE **MOST** WHITE HOUSE STATE DINNERS, AT 20 AS OF 2016.

**25**

In 2015, the State Dining Room was **REMODELED**—with custom-made **RUGS** and new **PAINT COLOR**—to the tune of $590,000.

# 15 WILD FACTS ABOUT

**1** President **Thomas Jefferson** had a **pet mockingbird** that flew freely around the White House.

**2** President **George Washington** insisted that his **horses** be **bathed** from head to toe and even had their **teeth brushed** before riding them.

**3** President **Herbert Hoover's** son's **pet alligators** crawled around the White House Grounds.

**4** President **Calvin Coolidge's** pets included dogs, a **donkey**, a **bobcat**, lion cubs, a bear, a wallaby, and a **pygmy hippo**.

**5** President Jefferson also kept two **grizzly bears**—given to him by explorer **Zebulon Pike**—which he took for walks around the White House gardens.

**6** President **Warren G. Harding** once threw a **birthday party** for his dog Laddie Boy, complete with doggie guests and a **frosted biscuit cake**.

**7** First Lady **Dolley Madison** would often entertain guests while walking around with her **pet parrot** perched on her shoulder.

# PRESIDENTIAL PETS

**8** President **Woodrow Wilson** kept a **herd of sheep** on the White House Lawn, auctioning off their wool to **raise money** for World War I efforts.

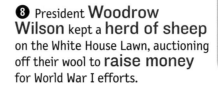

**9** President **Theodore Roosevelt's** daughter Alice kept a **pet garter snake** named Emily Spinach in the White House.

**10** President Roosevelt's son Quentin once tried to cheer up his sick brother Archie by bringing the family's pony into the elevator and to his room.

**11** When he moved into the **White House,** President William Howard Taft brought his pet cow, **Mooly Wooly,** so he could have fresh milk every day.

**12** President **Benjamin Harrison** had two **pet opossums** named Mr. Reciprocity and Mr. Protection.

**13** President **Martin Van Buren** once received **two tiger cubs** as a gift from the sultan of Oman. He later gave them to a zoo.

**14** After discovering a family of mice in his bedroom, President Andrew Johnson kept them as pets, leaving flour and water by the fireplace every night.

The Clintons' pet cat, Socks, peers over the lectern in the Press Briefing Room.

**15** President **Bill Clinton's** cat, **Socks,** was a stray adopted by his daughter, Chelsea, when he was governor of **Arkansas.** It was brought to the White House.

# 15 COLORFUL FACTS ABOUT

❶ There are more than **500 pieces of art** in the White House's permanent collection, including everything from **presidential portraits** to abstract paintings.

❷ The **White House curator** oversees the entire collection, while also working on acquiring **new art** and **artifacts**.

❸ Each president is allowed to **select the artwork** to line the walls of the private quarters in the White House Residence and Oval Office, including **portraits of their favorite predecessors**.

❹ Presidents can select items from a collection of **sculptures, drawings,** and famous **paintings,** many of which are kept in a White House storage area.

❺ Works of art owned by First Lady **Jacqueline Kennedy** that she used to decorate the White House were among her possessions sold at **auction** in 1996 for **$34,457,470.**

❻ Barack Obama borrowed items from the **National Museum of American History** to decorate the White House, including a **140-year-old steamboat paddle wheel.**

❼ A bust of **Martin Luther King, Jr.,** from the Smithsonian's National Portrait Gallery, has been displayed in the **Oval Office.**

# ART IN THE WHITE HOUSE

**8** During the **White House fire** in 1814, First Lady Dolley Madison famously saved a **full-length portrait** of **George Washington** before fleeing.

**9** The portrait of Washington is now hanging in the **East Room** of the White House.

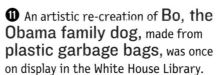

**10** A full-length portrait of **First Lady Grace Coolidge** wearing a red dress and posing with her dog hangs in the China Room.

**11** An artistic re-creation of **Bo, the Obama family dog,** made from **plastic garbage bags,** was once on display in the White House Library.

**12** During President Ulysses S. Grant's administration, the **public** could **visit the artwork** displayed in the White House's East Room.

**13** In August 1980, Gerald R. Ford attended the **unveiling** of a portrait of him as president in the **East Room.**

**The Green Room is filled with works of art.**

**14** Paintings by artistic presidents **George W. Bush** and **Dwight D. Eisenhower** are on display at **Blair House,** across from the White House.

**15** Today, you can go online and check out 360-degree digital tours of all of the art in the White House.

23

**1**
EARLY PRESIDENTS GOT AROUND ON **HORSES** AND KEPT THEM IN THE **EXECUTIVE STABLES** ON THE WHITE HOUSE GROUNDS.

**2**
Presidents including Ulysses S. Grant, Benjamin Harrison, Abraham Lincoln, and William McKinley traveled in open-air **HORSE-DRAWN CARRIAGES.**

**3**
There's a **TOP SECRET TRAIN** platform beneath the streets of **NEW YORK CITY** reserved just for presidential visits to the Big Apple.

**4**
In 1899, William McKinley became the first U.S. president to ride in a car, a steam-engine powered auto called the Stanley Steamer.

**5**
In 1909, President William Howard Taft bought the first two **CARS** for the White House, which included a **LIMOUSINE** for $12,000.

# 25 FAST FACTS ABOUT PRESIDENTIAL

**6**
PRESIDENT FRANKLIN D. ROOSEVELT TRAVELED IN A 1939 BLACK, STEEL-ARMORED CONVERTIBLE NICKNAMED THE "SUNSHINE SPECIAL."

**7**
In 1945, Franklin D. Roosevelt traveled to the Soviet Union on a **SPECIAL AIRPLANE** named *SACRED COW.*

**8**
Today, any plane with a president on board is called **AIR FORCE ONE,** also known as the "FLYING WHITE HOUSE."

**9**
PRESIDENT JOHN F. KENNEDY WAS THE FIRST PRESIDENT TO FLY REGULARLY ON **AIR FORCE ONE.**

**10**
President Lyndon B. Johnson's presidential plane was equipped with a **doggy door** so his beagles could roam about the cabin.

**13**
The *presidential motorcade*—a line of cars and motorcycles—includes a police escort, two *identical limousines,* and an ambulance.

**11**
THERE ARE ACTUALLY TWO AIR FORCE ONE PLANES, EACH WITH A BODY THAT CAN WITHSTAND A **NUCLEAR BLAST** FROM THE GROUND.

**12**
**Cargo planes** *typically fly ahead of Air Force One to provide the president with services needed in* **remote locations.**

**14** OTHER VEHICLES IN THE MOTORCADE CARRY STAFF MEMBERS, THE PRESIDENT'S **DOCTOR,** PHOTOGRAPHERS, AND **REPORTERS.**

**15** *The official presidential limousine is often* **TRANSPORTED OVERSEAS** *when the president is traveling* **ABROAD.**

**16** IN 2009, PRESIDENT BARACK OBAMA RODE TO HIS SWEARING-IN CEREMONY IN A **LIMO** NICKNAMED **"THE BEAST."**

**17** *President George W. Bush once traded his presidential limo for an* SUV *with the* PRESIDENTIAL SEAL *on the door.*

**18** PRESIDENT DWIGHT D. EISENHOWER WAS THE FIRST PRESIDENT TO USE A *private helicopter* THAT TOOK OFF AND LANDED ON THE *White House Lawn.*

# WHEELS AND WINGS

**19** The presidential helicopter, Marine One, accompanies the president wherever he travels and is built for rescue efforts during emergencies.

**20**

MARINE ONE CAN REACH **SPEEDS** OF 150 MILES AN HOUR (241 KM/H).

**21** *Any helicopter carrying the* VICE PRESIDENT *of the United States is called* MARINE TWO.

**25** In honor of Lincoln's 200th **BIRTHDAY,** President Obama took a similar **TRAIN RIDE** in 2009 from Philadelphia to Washington, D.C.

**22** A presidential **YACHT** now named the **U.S.S. *Sequoia*** served presidents from **1933** to **1977.**

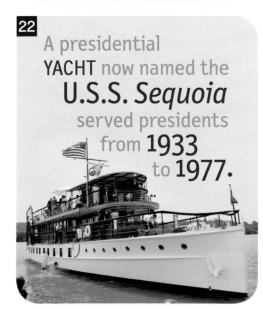

**23** PRESIDENT JOHN F. KENNEDY **OFTEN SAILED** HIS YACHT *HONEY FITZ* ON THE NEARBY **POTOMAC RIVER.**

**24** In February 1861, **ABRAHAM LINCOLN** took a train ride from Springfield, Illinois, to Washington, D.C., visiting supporters before his presidential Inauguration.

# 15 PLAYFUL FACTS ABOUT

❶ President Abraham Lincoln's son Tad rode around the grounds of the White House on a pony.

❷ In 1893, President Grover Cleveland's daughter Esther became the first child of a president to be born in the White House.

❸ President James A. Garfield's son Irvin took his bicycle for a spin down the White House's grand staircase and into the East Room. He did so without harming himself.

❹ Scott and Fanny Hayes, children of President Rutherford B. Hayes, played hide-and-seek with visiting dignitaries and senators in various White House rooms.

5 President Theodore Roosevelt's children roller-skated on the newly installed wood floors of the East Room.

❻ President Gerald R. Ford's son Jack took scuba-diving lessons in the White House pool.

❼ When John F. Kennedy became president in 1961, parents could celebrate his election by buying a doll modeled after his daughter, Caroline.

First daughter Susan Ford takes center stage during her school's prom, held in the East Room.

# WHITE HOUSE KIDS

**8** First son Steven Ford once blasted rock music while sitting on the roof of the White House.

**9** When they moved into the White House, Malia (then 10) and Sasha (then 7) Obama were the youngest children to live there in decades.

**10** President Calvin Coolidge's sons wrestled with lion cubs that their father received as a gift.

**11** It is said that first daughter Amy Carter was sent a chainsaw for Christmas in 1977 after she said she liked the way they work.

**12** President Donald J. Trump's son, Barron William Trump, is bilingual, fluent in both English and Slovenian.

**13** President Benjamin Harrison's grandchildren used to ride on a goat cart across the White House Lawn.

**14** President Ronald Reagan made snowmen on the White House Grounds with his grandchildren.

**15** First daughter Susan Ford held her school's senior prom in the East Room of the White House in 1975.

# 75 WEIRD BUT TRUE FACTS ABOUT THE

**1** President George Washington had dentures made of gold, hippo ivory, lead, and a cow's tooth—but not wood.

**2** HE PAID AROUND $15 FOR HIS DENTURES, ABOUT THE SAME AS WHAT THE AVERAGE WORKER MADE IN A MONTH AT THE TIME.

**3** In 1789, President Washington checked out two library books but never returned them. There is still a fine in his name.

**4** President Washington put out major fires at least twice in his life: once as a child and later just months before he died.

**5** President John Adams was not a studious child and sometimes skipped class to go fishing.

**6** President Adams had to use an outhouse since the White House had no indoor bathrooms or running water.

**7** As one of the founders of the United States and first U.S. ambassador to Great Britain, President Adams is nicknamed "The Father of American Independence."

**8** The *Jeffersonia diphylla* family of plants is named after President Thomas Jefferson.

**9** President Jefferson sometimes showed up to important meetings wearing his pajamas.

**10** At the time of his death, Jefferson was some $100,000 in debt—equivalent to about $2 million today.

**11** The smallest president, James Madison stood five feet four inches (160 cm) tall and weighed 100 pounds (45 kg).

**12** Without running water in the White House, President Madison bathed in a tub filled with water heated on a stove then transported in a bucket.

**13** President Madison is on the $5,000 bill, which is no longer printed.

**14** Three of the first five U.S. presidents—John Adams, Thomas Jefferson, and James Monroe—died on July 4.

**15** PRESIDENT JOHN QUINCY ADAMS WOULD OFTEN SKINNY-DIP IN A CREEK NEAR THE WHITE HOUSE.

**16** Revelers at a raging White House party during President Andrew Jackson's tenure broke dishes and stood on furniture in their muddy boots.

**17** President Jackson once invited the public into the White House to help him eat a 1,400-pound (635-kg) block of cheese he received as a gift.

**18** The resulting mob trampled so much cheese into the carpeting that it took months to remove the smell.

**19** President Martin Van Buren is often associated with the word "OK," a reference to his hometown of Old Kinderhook, New York. OK eventually came to mean "all right."

**20** PRESIDENT WILLIAM HENRY HARRISON WAS IN OFFICE FOR JUST 32 DAYS BEFORE HE DIED.

**21** President John Tyler aspired to be a concert violinist and often played for guests at the White House.

**22** At a Fourth of July dinner at the White House, President Tyler once served giant turtle soup. The 300-pound (136-kg) turtle had been caught at Key West, Florida.

**23** President Tyler had 15 children: eight with his first wife, Letitia, and seven more with his second wife, Julia.

**24** President Zachary Taylor may have died from eating a bowl of cherries contaminated with cholera, a deadly disease.

**25** President Abraham Lincoln was a champion wrestler and holds a spot in the Wrestling Hall of Fame.

**26** President Lincoln used to keep important documents in his top hat.

**27** He signed a law to create the Secret Service on the same day he was shot.

**28** President Lincoln owned a ring that contained a piece of George Washington's coffin.

**29** Long before he became president and entered the White House, Andrew Johnson was a tailor.

**30** President Johnson couldn't read until he was 14 and didn't learn to write until after he was married.

**31** Police stopped President Ulysses S. Grant three times for riding his horse and buggy too fast down the streets of Washington, D.C.

**32** PRESIDENT JAMES A. GARFIELD COULD WRITE IN GREEK WITH HIS LEFT HAND AND LATIN WITH HIS RIGHT AT THE SAME TIME.

**33** President Chester A. Arthur loved to fish and reportedly caught a massive 80-pound (36-kg) bass off the coast of Rhode Island during his tenure.

**34** Known for being fashionable, President Arthur owned 80 pairs of pants and changed the ones he wore a few times a day.

**35** To raise money for new decor, President Arthur sold old furniture and other items found around the White House.

**36** Grover Cleveland is the only president to be elected to two nonconsecutive terms. He was the 22nd and 24th president.

**37** President Benjamin Harrison had the White House wired for electricity in 1891 but never touched a switch. He was afraid of being electrocuted.

# PRESIDENTS

**38** President William McKinley wore a single red carnation in his suit lapel every day.

**39** Teddy bears are named after President Theodore "Teddy" Roosevelt, who once refused to shoot a bear cub.

**40** THEODORE ROOSEVELT WORE A RING WITH A LOCK OF ABRAHAM LINCOLN'S HAIR IN IT TO HIS INAUGURATION IN 1905.

**41** President William Howard Taft, who weighed more than 300 pounds (136 kg), had a special tub built in his White House bathroom that was big enough to fit four average-size men.

**42** He also built a sleeping porch on the roof of the White House in order to beat the heat.

**43** Like Lincoln, President Taft was a top wrestler, winning a championship in the heavyweight division in college.

**44** President Woodrow Wilson played more than 1,000 rounds of golf while in office, more than any other president in history.

**45** President Warren G. Harding wore a size 14 shoe—the largest shoe size of any U.S. president.

**46** President Harding is credited with coining the term "Founding Fathers" in 1916.

**47** President Calvin Coolidge kept an electric horse inside the White House so he could practice trotting and galloping.

**48** He often ate breakfast while an aide massaged Vaseline into his scalp.

**49** President Coolidge routinely slept 11 hours a night—and took long naps during the day.

**50** With no security guards in sight, President Coolidge was known to take walks by himself through Washington, D.C.

**51** President Herbert Hoover's staff was ordered to hide from him whenever he passed by—or risk being fired.

**52** PRESIDENT FRANKLIN D. ROOSEVELT WAS THE FIFTH COUSIN OF THEODORE ROOSEVELT AND MARRIED HIS NIECE, ELEANOR.

**53** President Franklin D. Roosevelt was the first president whose mother was able to vote for him.

**54** The S in President Harry S. Truman's name stands for the names of both his grandfathers.

**55** President Lyndon B. Johnson named his daughters Luci Baines and Lynda Bird and his dog Little Beagle Johnson after his own "LBJ" initials.

**56** In 1970, Elvis Presley and President Richard M. Nixon met in the Oval Office.

**57** President Nixon was the first president to visit all 50 U.S. states—and the first to visit China.

**58** Before entering politics, President Gerald R. Ford was a model and appeared on the cover of a fashion magazine.

**59** President Ford received offers from two professional football teams, the Detroit Lions and the Green Bay Packers, but turned them down to pursue law school.

**60** As a nod to his background as a peanut farmer, President Jimmy Carter had a giant peanut-shaped balloon float as part of his Inaugural parade.

**61** President Carter once claimed to have seen a UFO flying in the night skies.

**62** President Carter wrote a children's book called *The Little Baby Snoogle-Fleejer.*

**63** President Carter is said to be able to speed-read more than 2,000 words a minute.

**64** PRESIDENT RONALD REAGAN KEPT A JAR OF JELLY BEANS ON THE TABLE AT CABINET MEETINGS.

**65** One of President Reagan's traditions was to feed the squirrels outside of the Oval Office with acorns he collected from Camp David.

**66** President Reagan once starred in a movie about an anthropologist raising a chimp like a child.

**67** PRESIDENT GEORGE H. W. BUSH NAMED HIS DOG, RANGER, AFTER HIS FAVORITE PROFESSIONAL BASEBALL TEAM.

**68** As president, Bill Clinton reportedly sent just two emails. He preferred to write letters or talk on the phone.

**69** Before vacating the White House for the George W. Bush team, President Clinton's aides are said to have pulled off the *W* key from a computer keyboard.

**70** Presidents Clinton and George H. W. Bush are the only consecutive presidents who were left-handed.

**71** President George W. Bush was his high school's head cheerleader.

**72** George W. Bush is the only president to have run a marathon.

**73** President Barack Obama read every Harry Potter book with his daughter Malia.

**74** President Obama appeared in a Spider-Man comic book, where the superhero saves him during an Inauguration event.

**75** Prior to becoming president, Donald J. Trump hosted the hit TV reality show *The Apprentice.*

**1**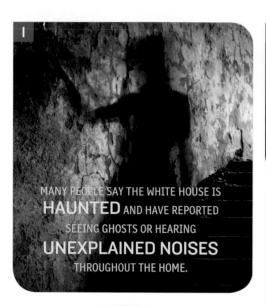
MANY PEOPLE SAY THE WHITE HOUSE IS **HAUNTED** AND HAVE REPORTED SEEING GHOSTS OR HEARING **UNEXPLAINED NOISES** THROUGHOUT THE HOME.

**2** Mary Lincoln, President Abraham Lincoln's wife, held **séances** to channel spirits in the White House.

**3** LEGEND HAS IT THAT THE GHOST OF PRESIDENT LINCOLN **HAUNTS** THE **LINCOLN BEDROOM.**

**4** When he stayed in the **LINCOLN BEDROOM,** British prime minister Winston Churchill claimed to see Lincoln's ghost **APPEAR** by the **FIREPLACE.**

**5** During her stay, the queen of the Netherlands reportedly **FAINTED** after the ghost of Abraham Lincoln **KNOCKED** on her **BEDROOM DOOR.**

# 25 SPOOKY AND SCARY FACTS ABOUT THE

**6** LADY BIRD JOHNSON, WIFE OF PRESIDENT LYNDON B. JOHNSON, TOLD OF FEELING LINCOLN'S PRESENCE WHILE **WATCHING A TV SHOW** ABOUT HIM.

**7** A ROOM USED BY MANY FIRST FAMILIES AS A **PRIVATE DINING** SPACE IS THE SAME ROOM WHERE **PRESIDENT WILLIAM HENRY HARRISON** DIED IN 1841.

**8** IT'S ALSO THE ROOM WHERE PRESIDENT LINCOLN'S **AUTOPSY** AND **EMBALMING** TOOK PLACE.

**9** AIDES TO BOTH PRESIDENTS FRANKLIN D. ROOSEVELT AND WILLIAM HOWARD TAFT REPORTED HEARING A **MYSTERIOUS VOICE** SAYING "I'M MR. BURNS" IN THE **YELLOW OVAL ROOM.**

**10** THE VOICE IS BELIEVED TO BELONG TO David Burnes, THE original owner OF SOME OF THE FARMLAND ON WHICH THE WHITE HOUSE WAS BUILT.

**13** THE GHOST OF FIRST LADY DOLLEY MADISON APPARENTLY APPEARED IN THE WHITE HOUSE **ROSE GARDEN,** SCOLDING **GARDENERS** FOR DIGGING UP HER **ROSE BUSHES.**

**11** First daughter LYNDA JOHNSON said she was once visited by the GHOST of President Lincoln's son WILLIE, who died at age 12.

**12** **CHARLIE TAFT,** son of President William Howard Taft, took his **GUESTS** on **GHOST TOURS** in the White House.

**14** The ghost of First Lady **ABIGAIL ADAMS** —wearing a cap and a lace shawl—has supposedly been seen in the **EAST ROOM** hanging laundry.

**15** It is said that the ghost of an angry President **ANDREW JACKSON** haunts the **QUEENS' BEDROOM.**

**16** The **QUEENS' BEDROOM,** Jackson's bedroom while he was president, is said to be one of the **MOST HAUNTED** White House locations.

**17** SOME PEOPLE CLAIM TO HAVE SEEN THE **GHOST** OF PRESIDENT WILLIAM HENRY HARRISON **RUMMAGING** AROUND THE **ATTIC.**

**18** PRESIDENT **HARRY S. TRUMAN** WROTE LETTERS TO HIS WIFE, BESS, ABOUT **GHOSTS** IN HIS STUDY AND HEARING THE **DRAPES MOVE** BACK AND FORTH.

# WHITE HOUSE

**19** BOTH PRESIDENTS FRANKLIN D. ROOSEVELT'S SON AND HARRY S. TRUMAN'S DAUGHTER **WROTE MURDER MYSTERIES** ABOUT WASHINGTON, D.C., AFTER LIVING IN THE WHITE HOUSE.

**20** Jenna Bush, daughter of President George W. Bush, once heard **OPERA MUSIC** blaring from a **FIREPLACE** in her room at night.

**21** **GATE RATTLING** and **WEEPING** heard in the White House are said to be from the ghost of a **YOUNG WOMAN** whose mother was killed in 1865.

**22** THE REAGAN FAMILY'S DOG, **REX,** WOULD **BARK** FRANTICALLY OUTSIDE OF THE DOOR TO THE **LINCOLN** BEDROOM, BUT NEVER WENT INSIDE.

**23** People have reported seeing the spirit of President John Tyler in the **BLUE ROOM, PROPOSING** to his second wife, **JULIA.**

**24** AN UNNAMED **BRITISH SOLDIER** WHO DIED DURING THE **WAR OF 1812** IS SAID TO LURK AROUND THE GROUNDS OF THE WHITE HOUSE, **HOLDING A TORCH.**

**25** THE SPIRIT OF A **TEENAGE BOY** KNOWN AS **THE THING** IS SAID TO HAVE HAUNTED THE WHITE HOUSE WHILE PRESIDENT TAFT LIVED THERE.

# 15 FESTIVE FACTS ABOUT

**1** Each year, the official White House **Christmas tree** is placed in the **Blue Room.**

**2** There are often as many as 50 other **Christmas trees** displayed throughout the house during the holiday season.

**3** A White House pastry chef once made a **500-pound (227-kg) gingerbread** replica of the White House.

**4** President Theodore Roosevelt once tried to ban **Christmas trees** from the White House in an effort to **prevent deforestation.**

**5** **Roosevelt's** plan backfired after his children **snuck live Christmas trees** into the White House and **decorated them** on their own.

**6** President **Franklin Pierce** decorated the **first Christmas tree** on the White House Lawn in 1853.

**7** Before the White House had **electricity,** the first family would decorate their Christmas tree with **candles and toys.**

President John F. Kennedy and his family celebrate Christmas Day at the White House in 1962.

# CHRISTMAS IN THE WHITE HOUSE

8 The White House hosted an annual holiday **3D-Printed Ornament** Challenge. The winners went on display at the Smithsonian's National Museum of American History.

**9** President Andrew Jackson once hosted an elaborate **children's Christmas party,** which ended with an indoor **"snowball fight"** using cotton balls.

**10** Some **70,000 people** visit the White House each year during the holiday season.

**11** In 1903, President Theodore Roosevelt threw a **holiday carnival** for 500 children, complete with **Santa-shaped ice cream.**

**12** President Calvin Coolidge lit the first **National Christmas Tree** in 1923, a tradition that continues today.

**13** **Barney,** the first dog during the George W. Bush administration, led a **video "tour"** of the White House during the holidays.

**14** President **Franklin D. Roosevelt** had a tradition of reading Charles Dickens's *A Christmas Carol* to his family on Christmas Eve.

**15** In 2015, one of the White House Christmas trees featured **doggy treats and tennis ball ornaments,** a nod to the Obamas' dogs, Bo and Sunny.

**❶** Many presidential guests stay at **Blair House** across the street from the White House.

**❷** President Franklin D. Roosevelt arranged the purchase of the 14-bedroom Blair House in 1942 as a place for **heads of state** to stay while visiting the president.

**³ Blair House** staff stock the fridge with its guests' favorite foods, like **hamburgers** for the king of Jordan and **borscht ice cream** for a Russian leader.

**❹** During a **foreign leader's stay**, the **flag of his or her nation flies** over Blair House.

**❺** In 1941, British prime minister **Winston Churchill** had a **24-day stay** at the White House.

**❻** First Lady **Eleanor Roosevelt** once found Churchill **wandering the halls** of the White House at 3 a.m. during his visit.

**❼** Legendary British writer **Charles Dickens** dined with President **John Tyler** at the White House in 1842.

**President Nelson Mandela of South Africa sits with President George W. Bush in the White House.**

# WHITE HOUSE GUESTS

**8** In 1957, President Dwight D. Eisenhower hosted **Queen Elizabeth II** and **Prince Philip** for a four-day stay at the White House.

**9** The White House is also known as the **People's House,** as guests from **around the world** are welcome to tour the home during designated hours.

**10** Former South African president **Nelson Mandela** visited the White House several times, most recently in 2005.

**11** In 2015, First Lady Michelle Obama hosted **a sleepover for 50 Girl Scouts** on the White House Lawn.

**12** President Bill Clinton once hosted former **president Jimmy Carter** and **11 of his family members** for an overnight stay in the White House.

**13** In 2009, the White House began publicly posting records of all visitors for the first time in history.

**14** Public tours of the White House take visitors only through the **East Wing** and **State Floors** of the residence.

**15** Of the **938 overnight guests** who visited the Clintons between 1993 and 1996, 821 of them slept in the **Lincoln Bedroom.**

# 15 GREEN FACTS ABOUT THE

**1** President Lyndon B. Johnson earned the nickname **"Light Bulb Johnson"** for his vigilance in **turning off lights** in the house to save energy.

**2** In 1979, **President Jimmy Carter** installed **solar panels** on the roof of the West Wing to **heat** the home's **water supply.**

**3** Today, **solar panels** cover a portion of the White House roof, generating enough **energy to run an average-size home.**

**4** The White House's **hot tub, outdoor shower,** and **pool** are heated by solar energy.

**5** The **100-year-old lanterns** in the White House portico are outfitted with **eco-friendly LED lights.**

**6** During his administration, President Bill Clinton saved more than **$1.4 million in electricity bills** by using energy-efficient windows, light bulbs, and heating.

**7** In 2001, President George W. Bush proclaimed November 15 as **America Recycles Day,** encouraging people to reduce waste.

**8** The White House Grounds include a **garden** with **55** varieties of vegetables and fruits, and a beehive.

# ECO-FRIENDLY WHITE HOUSE

First Lady Michelle Obama and local schoolchildren harvest the White House vegetable garden.

**9** **Millions of trees** were planted around the country as part of President Franklin D. Roosevelt's **New Deal** to boost the country's economy and environment.

**10** The White House **garden** is regularly fertilized with **compost** made from **food scraps** and **yard waste** from the house.

**11** Upon moving into the White House, the Obamas set up a **swing set made out of recycled materials,** including bouncy flooring out of repurposed tires.

**12** The **White House Easter Egg Roll** features eggs made from eco-friendly wood and vegetable-oil-based inks.

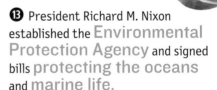

**13** President Richard M. Nixon established the **Environmental Protection Agency** and signed bills **protecting the oceans** and **marine life.**

**14** The **White House Christmas tree** is lit with LED lights. After the festivities, the **ornaments** are usually given to the **presidential libraries.**

**15** **Low-flush toilets** have been installed in the White House to save water.

**1** UNTIL 1850, ALL COOKING IN THE WHITE HOUSE WAS DONE OVER AN OPEN FLAME.

**2** DURING HIS ADMINISTRATION, PRESIDENT MILLARD FILLMORE UPDATED THE WHITE HOUSE AND INSTALLED THE **FIRST IRON STOVE** IN THE KITCHEN.

**3** PRESIDENT THOMAS JEFFERSON WAS SO FOND OF **FRANCE** THAT HE HIRED A **FRENCH CHEF** TO SERVE MEALS IN THE WHITE HOUSE.

**4** After requesting "potatoes served in the French manner" for an 1802 White House dinner, Jefferson **INTRODUCED FRENCH FRIES** to America.

**5** Jefferson was also the first to serve **ICE CREAM** and **MACARONI AND CHEESE** to American guests while in the White House.

**6** President Abraham Lincoln's favorite foods included **CORN BREAD** drizzled with honey and **PECAN PIE**.

# 25 DELECTABLE FACTS ABOUT

**7** After discovering **COCKROACHES** in the White House kitchen during a tour in 1933, First Lady **ELEANOR ROOSEVELT** requested a total renovation.

**8** TODAY THE STATE-OF-THE-ART WHITE HOUSE KITCHEN HAS THE CAPACITY TO COOK DINNER FOR **140 GUESTS,** AND **APPETIZERS** FOR UP TO **1,000.**

**9** The White House kitchen staff includes **FIVE FULL-TIME CHEFS.**

**10** The **FIRST** White House **EXECUTIVE CHEF** was appointed by First Lady Jacqueline Kennedy in 1961 and made a salary of about $10,000 a year.

**11** TODAY, THE WHITE HOUSE EXECUTIVE CHEF EARNS **A SIX-FIGURE SALARY.**

**13** The White House's **MEZZANINE PANTRY** includes a kitchen dedicated to **JUST SWEETS.**

**12** THE WHITE HOUSE EXECUTIVE **pastry chef** BECAME A PERMANENT POSITION IN **1979.**

**14**

Henry Haller, the **LONGEST RUNNING** White House executive chef, cooked for **FIVE PRESIDENTS** from 1966 to 1987.

**15**

PRESIDENT DWIGHT D. EISENHOWER WAS A **SKILLED COOK** AND SHARED SOME OF HIS **RECIPES** WITH THE WHITE HOUSE CHEF FOR FORMAL DINNERS.

**16**

The menu for a White House press corps' party in the 1930s included **25 HAMS** and 10 pounds (4.5 kg) of a variety of **COLD CUTS.**

**17**

A 2007 White House dinner for ENGLAND'S QUEEN ELIZABETH featured a FIVE-COURSE menu including pea soup, spring lamb, and petits fours for dessert.

# FOOD IN THE WHITE HOUSE

**18**

IT'S SAID THAT PRESIDENT GEORGE H. W. BUSH WOULD OFTEN **POP** INTO THE WHITE HOUSE KITCHEN TO **SNACK AND CHAT.**

**19**

First Lady Jacqueline Kennedy created a small **KITCHEN** and **DINING ROOM** on the second floor of the house so the family could enjoy meals in a **CASUAL SETTING.**

**20**

Lyndon and Lady Bird Johnson liked to eat off of trays **IN FRONT OF THE TV** while watching their **FAVORITE SHOW.**

**21**

Lyndon B. Johnson had a **DRINK MACHINE** installed in a White House lounge so he could get a **SODA DRINK** on demand.

**22**

Not a fan of **BROCCOLI,** President George H. W. Bush reportedly **BANNED** the veggie from the White House and Air Force One.

**23**

At the 2014 state dinner for the president of France, caviar, **QUAIL EGGS,** and 12 kinds of **POTATOES** were served.

**24**

DURING THE 1960s AND 1970s, THE **PRESIDENTIAL PASTRY CHEF** PREPARED UP TO **180 FRUITCAKES** A YEAR FOR WHITE HOUSE **HOLIDAY PARTIES.**

**25**

THE WHITE HOUSE CHEF GAVE FIRST DAUGHTER CHELSEA CLINTON AND HER FRIENDS COOKING LESSONS BEFORE CHELSEA LEFT FOR COLLEGE.

39

**1** In the early 1900s, President Theodore Roosevelt established the first White House **PRESS ROOM,** giving reporters a **DESIGNATED** space in the West Wing.

**2** PRESIDENT WOODROW WILSON HELD THE FIRST **PRESIDENTIAL PRESS CONFERENCES** AT THE WHITE HOUSE IN 1913.

**3** President John F. Kennedy's **PRESS CONFERENCES** were the first to be shown on **LIVE TV.**

**4** IN THE 1960s, REPORTERS WOULD **lounge on couches** IN THE **West Wing lobby** AND TALK TO WHITE HOUSE VISITORS.

**5** President Richard M. Nixon introduced **PRIME-TIME** press conferences as a way to generate more interest from the **PUBLIC.**

# 25 VOCAL FACTS ABOUT PRESIDENTIAL

**6** TRANSCRIPTS OF ALL PRESS CONFERENCES, AS WELL AS **speeches** GIVEN BY THE PRESIDENT AND THE FIRST LADY, ARE POSTED **online.**

**7** PRESIDENT NIXON OVERSAW THE CONSTRUCTION OF A **PRESS BRIEFING ROOM** ABOVE AN OLD **INDOOR POOL** TO ACCOMMODATE A GROWING NEWS CREW.

**8** TV REPORTERS often report from "STONEHENGE"—part of the NORTH LAWN that's covered with flagstone and offers a backdrop of the White House.

**9** In 2007, the Press Briefing Room reopened after an **EIGHT MILLION DOLLAR RENOVATION** to **IMPROVE TECHNOLOGY** and replace outdated fixtures.

**10** The White House PRESS SECRETARY is the primary SPOKESPERSON for the president's ADMINISTRATION.

**11** An **OFF-CAMERA, INFORMAL** briefing by the press secretary is called a **GAGGLE.**

**12** THERE ARE **PRESS BRIEFINGS** AT THE WHITE HOUSE ALMOST EVERY **WEEKDAY.**

**13**

President Gerald R. Ford once **SWAM LAPS** in the new outdoor White House pool while the **PRESS** photographed him.

**14** PRESIDENT ABRAHAM LINCOLN GAVE HIS **FINAL SPEECH** BEFORE HIS DEATH IN 1865 FROM A SECOND FLOOR WINDOW TO THE PUBLIC STANDING ON THE WHITE HOUSE **LAWN**.

**17** ONLY ONE **PHOTOGRAPHER** IS PERMITTED TO **TAKE PICTURES** OF THE PRESIDENT DURING A WHITE HOUSE SPEECH.

**16** WARREN G. HARDING WAS THE FIRST PRESIDENT TO **DELIVER A SPEECH** FROM THE WHITE HOUSE **ON THE RADIO**.

**15** The president often makes speeches and announcements from the steps to the White House **ROSE GARDEN**, located outside the **OVAL OFFICE**.

# INTERVIEWS AND SPEECHES

**18** PRESIDENT FRANKLIN D. ROOSEVELT'S RADIO SPEECHES BECAME KNOWN AS **FIRESIDE CHATS** BECAUSE OF THEIR **CONVERSATIONAL** TONE.

**19** In 1947, President Harry S. Truman gave the first televised address from the Oval Office.

**20** SINCE THEN, U.S. PRESIDENTS HAVE GIVEN MANY OF THEIR MOST **IMPORTANT** TELEVISED **ADDRESSES** FROM THE OVAL OFFICE.

**21** RONALD REAGAN GAVE **34** SPEECHES FROM THE OVAL OFFICE, THE **MOST** OF ANY PRESIDENT.

**22** President Nixon gave nearly 25 addresses from the Oval Office, including his **RESIGNATION SPEECH IN 1974**.

**23** Eleanor Roosevelt made more than **300 RADIO APPEARANCES** during her time in the White House, earning her the nickname **"THE FIRST LADY OF RADIO."**

**24** PRESIDENT GEORGE W. BUSH WAS THE FIRST **CHIEF EXECUTIVE** TO OFFER HIS REGULAR PUBLIC ADDRESS AS A **PODCAST**.

**25** President Barack Obama introduced a weekly ONLINE VIDEO address and began posting his speeches on YOUTUBE.

41

**1**
A 1961 act of Congress declared all historic White House artifacts part of a permanent museum collection.

**2**
The White House has a collection of about 30,000 historic objects, including paintings, furniture, and historic documents.

**3**
First Lady Jacqueline Kennedy redecorated the state rooms in the White House using historic objects and American antiques.

**4**
The China Room displays examples of not only historic china but also glassware and silver.

**5**
In the 19th century, the president's china was frequently sold at auction or given away once an administration was over.

**6**
White House staff once smashed dessert plates made for President Lyndon B. Johnson against a wall when they arrived flawed.

**7**
The wooden chandelier hanging in the White House library is more than 215 years old.

**8**
One of the many official china collections includes President Rutherford B. Hayes's set featuring American animals and plants.

**9**
Of the 269 pieces of china President Franklin Pierce purchased at the 1853 World's Fair in New York City, only a small number remain intact at the White House.

**10**
President Theodore Roosevelt's Nobel Peace Prize and Congressional Medal of Honor are displayed in a glass case in the Roosevelt Room.

**11**
First Lady Nancy Reagan spent a reported $200,000 on her signature White House china.

**12**
Since President Woodrow Wilson, all White House china has been made in America. Prior to that, the sets were brought from France or England.

**13**
In 1882, President Chester A. Arthur had a huge red, white, and blue screen made of valuable stained glass installed in the Entrance Hall.

**14**
The screen remained until it was taken down during the Theodore Roosevelt renovation in 1902 and sold at auction.

**15**
It's believed that the screen was later placed in a hotel in Maryland and destroyed when the building burned down in 1922.

**16**
President Roosevelt displayed huge moose heads over the State Dining Room mantel. (President Warren G. Harding later removed them.)

**17**
Roosevelt also had images of bison carved into the State Dining Room's mantelpiece to reflect the treasured American animal.

**18**
A series of four drawings by famous American artist Norman Rockwell hang on the walls of the West Wing.

**19**
There's a copy of President Abraham Lincoln's famous Gettysburg Address on display in the White House's Lincoln Bedroom.

**20**
The three giant chandeliers hanging in the East Room—featuring more than 6,000 pieces of cut glass—are hand-cleaned each year.

**21**
A centuries-old silver coffee urn once used by President John Adams sits on a table in the White House Green Room.

**22**
President Andrew Jackson sold old White House furniture in an auction to buy expensive tableware.

**23**
Some of the items President Jackson bought included a coffee set from Russia, which he had engraved with the words "President's House."

**24**
On special occasions, a 14-foot (4.3-m)-long mirrored and bronze centerpiece called a plateau decorates the State Dining Room table.

**25**
A pair of vases purchased by President James Monroe and featuring Benjamin Franklin's home in France still sit on the mantel in the Blue Room.

**26**
First Lady Julia Grant bought another centerpiece called Hiawatha's Boat in 1876 to mark the 100th anniversary of the signing of the Declaration of Independence.

**27**
The piece—featuring a silver boat on a mirrored "lake"—can still be viewed in the White House.

**28**
A silver soup tureen from the Monroe era is engraved with eagles, reflecting Monroe's patriotism and confidence in his young country as a world power.

**29**
Until the 20th century, the White House silver was stored in custom-made trunks. Later, a pantry was built to store the silver.

**30**
A wooden clock dating back to 1805 and measuring as tall as an elephant stands in the Oval Office.

# 50 PRICELESS Facts About White House TREASURES

Green Room eagle

**46**
Priceless presidential documents are tucked away in a 250-year-old mahogany bookcase in the West Wing Reception Room.

**31**
The bronze **Minerva clock**, purchased from France by President Monroe in 1817, strikes every hour and quarter hour in the **Blue Room.**

**34**
A **portrait of George Washington** has been in the White House collection longer than any other item.

**38**
An **eagle ornament** that topped the **White House flagpole** in the late 19th century is on display at the White House Visitor Center.

**42**
In 1862, the **king of Siam** offered President Lincoln a **herd of elephants** to populate U.S. forests. (Lincoln kindly refused.)

**47**
In 2013, the **queen of Brunei** gave First Lady Michelle Obama **jewelry** worth some **$70,000.**

**32**
President Herbert Hoover and his wife, Lou, brought many extravagant items like **pricey rugs** and **exotic birds** when they moved into the White House in 1929.

**35**
Washington's portrait is likely the last of **four identical versions** painted by **Gilbert Stuart** in the **1790s.**

**39**
In the 1970s, the White House **paid $21,600** for a 130-person set of **sterling silverware,** still used for formal meals.

**43**
The U.S. Constitution **prohibits the president from accepting expensive gifts** from foreign sources.

**48**
In 2001, the staff gave First Lady Hillary Clinton **a pillow made from fabric** she'd selected to **decorate different rooms** in the White House.

**33**
First Lady Hillary Clinton had a room in the White House where she stored memorabilia from fellow first lady **Eleanor Roosevelt.**

**36**
President John F. Kennedy kept a souvenir **coconut shell** as a **paperweight** on his Oval Office desk.

**40**
For decades, **foreign dignitaries** have showered presidents with **extravagant presents** during their visits to the White House.

**44**
Any gift valued at more than $375 is **stored away** or **put on display,** and the president has the option of buying it back when he leaves office.

**49**
The White House Historical Association issues a new **Christmas ornament each year.**

**37**
The paperweight was a **memento** from his time serving in the Pacific Ocean in **World War II.**

**41**
The pricey gifts are looked upon as a sign of **respect and admiration** for the president and the first family.

**45**
In 2015, a Saudi Arabian king gave President Barack Obama and his family more than **$1.3 million worth of gifts,** including watches and jewelry.

**50**
Hundreds of thousands of the ornaments are sold each year, with the money helping to maintain the public rooms in the house.

**1** President William Henry Harrison gave the longest ever Inauguration speech—ONE HOUR, 45 MINUTES—while standing in the pouring rain.

**2** AT JUST 135 WORDS LONG, PRESIDENT GEORGE WASHINGTON'S INAUGURAL ADDRESS IS THE SHORTEST IN HISTORY.

**3** In 1801, Thomas Jefferson became the **FIRST PRESIDENT** to take his presidential **OATH** in Washington, D.C.

**4** PRESIDENT JEFFERSON'S SECOND INAUGURATION, IN 1805, FEATURED THE **FIRST INAUGURAL PARADE.**

**5** President Harry S. Truman's lavish 1949 Inauguration—the first to be covered on live TV—featured a **FANCY GALA** and **FIREWORKS.**

# 25 EXCITING FACTS ABOUT THE PRESIDENTIAL

**6** IN 1809, PRESIDENT JAMES MADISON HELD THE FIRST OFFICIAL **INAUGURAL BALL,** WITH ADMISSION COSTING **FOUR DOLLARS PER TICKET.**

**7** ON MARCH 6, 1865, SOME OF THE 4,000 PEOPLE WHO ATTENDED PRESIDENT ABRAHAM LINCOLN'S SECOND INAUGURAL BALL DANCED UNTIL DAWN.

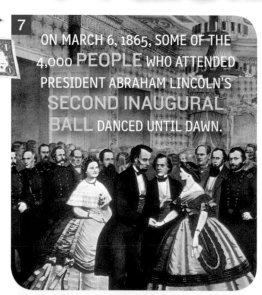

**8** In 1825, John Quincy Adams became the first president to wear **LONG PANTS,** instead of **KNEE BREECHES,** for his swearing in.

**9** President Franklin Pierce was the first to RECITE his entire Inaugural SPEECH from MEMORY, without any notes.

**10** President Calvin Coolidge—who became the 30th president after the unexpected death of Warren G. Harding—was SWORN IN BY HIS FATHER at his family's farmhouse.

**11** In recent years, Inaugural Ball tickets have been sold for as much as $12,500.

**12** PRESIDENT COOLIDGE'S 1925 INAUGURAL SPEECH WAS **BROADCAST** ON **21 RADIO STATIONS,** A FIRST FOR THE WHITE HOUSE.

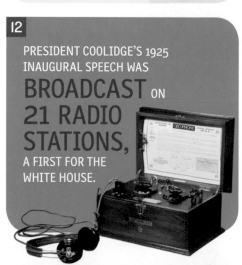

**13** President Franklin D. Roosevelt was the first president **SWORN INTO** office in **JANUARY.** Prior to that, Inaugurals were in **MARCH.**

**14** Worried about **ASSASSINATION THREATS,** President Lincoln **TRAVELED UNDERCOVER** to Washington D.C., for his Inauguration.

**15** President Bill Clinton's 1997 Inaugural speech was the first to be **BROADCAST LIVE** on the **INTERNET.**

**16** DURING HIS 1953 INAUGURATION, TEXAS-BORN PRESIDENT DWIGHT D. EISENHOWER WAS **LASSOED** BY A **COWBOY** WHO RODE UP TO HIM ON HORSEBACK.

**17** ONLY TWO PRESIDENTS —THOMAS JEFFERSON AND JIMMY CARTER— HAVE **WALKED** FROM THE **CAPITOL** TO THE **WHITE HOUSE** DURING THE INAUGURAL PARADE.

**18** On the morning of the Inauguration ceremony, the president-elect traditionally **WORSHIPS** at a **LOCAL CHURCH.**

# INAUGURATION

**19** For his Inauguration in 1921, Warren G. Harding became the first president to **RIDE TO AND FROM** the Capitol in a **CAR.**

**20** AN INAUGURATION DAY RECORD OF **10 INCHES (25 CM)** OF **SNOW** FELL AS PRESIDENT WILLIAM HOWARD TAFT WAS SWORN INTO OFFICE IN 1909.

**21**

PRESIDENT FRANKLIN D. ROOSEVELT FAMOUSLY **STOOD** IN THE FREEZING RAIN FOR AN HOUR AND A HALF DURING HIS SECOND INAUGURAL PARADE IN 1937.

**22** A RECORD-SETTING **1.8 MILLION PEOPLE** FLOODED THE STREETS OF WASHINGTON, D.C., FOR PRESIDENT BARACK OBAMA'S FIRST INAUGURATION IN 2009.

**23** George Washington **DINED ALONE** after his Inauguration in 1789.

**24** For decades, it was tradition for presidents to wear **TOP HATS** to their swearing in.

**25** IN 1997, BILL CLINTON AND HIS WIFE, HILLARY, ATTENDED 14 INAUGURAL BALLS IN ONE NIGHT—AN ALL-TIME HIGH FOR A PRESIDENT.

1. The White House is one of the oldest continuous residences in the world for a head of state.

2. In 1790, a Congress vote allowed for the construction of a home and office for the president in the nation's new capital city of Washington, D.C.

3. Even though he never lived in the White House, President George Washington selected the future site of the home overlooking the Potomac River.

4. Thomas Jefferson created a contest for architects and builders to design the White House.

5. **HE ADVERTISED THE CONTEST IN NEWSPAPERS, OFFERING $500 OR A GOLD MEDAL TO THE WINNER.**

6. Irish-born architect James Hoban won the contest, basing his design on a building in Dublin.

7. Jefferson himself submitted a design for the White House, but his plan was not chosen.

8. Construction began in 1792, with a plan for a neo-classical, federal-style home, built of light gray sandstone.

9. The sandstone was then sealed with paint mixed with salt, rice, and glue—to protect the stones from freezing in cold weather.

10. **THE PAINTING PROCESS, KNOWN AS WHITEWASHING, GAVE THE HOUSE ITS SIGNATURE COLOR.**

11. African-American workmen, both enslaved and free, were among those who worked on the construction of the White House in the late 1790s.

12. More than 220 years ago, Scottish stonemasons carved intricate roses and acorns above the White House north door. They are still visible now.

13. The White House was first designed to be five times bigger than today's mansion, but President Washington opted for a smaller home.

14. The stone walls seen today in the front of the house are those of the original building.

15. When President John Adams moved into the White House in 1800, about half of the 36 rooms were complete.

16. Upon moving into the White House, First Lady Abigail Adams described the unfinished home as cold and damp.

17. President Adams's family lived there for just five months before Thomas Jefferson became president in 1800.

18. The entire construction of the White House took almost 10 years to complete.

19. At first, President Jefferson refused to live in the White House, calling it too big and fancy for his taste.

20. President Jefferson eventually relented, and even added extensions to the east and west sides of the mansion.

21. **HE ALSO BUILT THE FIRST TOILETS IN THE UPPER FLOOR TO REPLACE THE OUTHOUSE.**

22. President Jefferson created a wilderness museum in the White House Entrance Hall, with mounted animals on display.

23. At the time, anyone was free to stroll the White House Grounds and enter the mansion to check out the museum.

24. It's said that in the 1820s a man parked his horse in front of the White House and walked in to shake President James Monroe's hand.

25. The White House kitchen was originally located in the basement—then an area also used as quarters for servants.

26. After a fire during the War of 1812 all but gutted the White House, President James Madison had the home rebuilt following George Washington's original plans.

27. President Monroe added the South Portico of the house in 1824, and President Andrew Jackson added the North Portico in 1830.

28. In the early years of the White House, some presidents kept their offices open to the public.

29. People would often flood the White House seeking jobs in the government.

30. In the 1840s, President James K. Polk hired an usher to meet guests at the White House door and take them to appointments—a position that's still important today.

31. Until 1850, Washington, D.C., had no sewer system, so human waste would sit in a stagnant marsh near the White House.

32. **DURING THE CIVIL WAR, SOLDIERS MARCHED ON THE WHITE HOUSE'S SOUTH LAWN AND CAMPED IN THE EAST ROOM.**

33. President Abraham Lincoln also held weekly band concerts on the lawn during the war.

34. Mourning the loss of their 11-year-old son, Willie, the Lincolns cancelled the popular performances in 1862.

35. To get war news, President Lincoln had to walk next door to the War Department because the White House wasn't equipped with a telegraph.

36. President Lincoln effectively ended slavery after signing the Emancipation Proclamation on January 1, 1863, in his White House study.

# 75 TIMELESS FACTS ABOUT WHITE HOUSE

**37** After President Lincoln's assassination in 1865, thousands of mourners viewed his body in the White House.

**38** Some of the visiting mourners walked away with valuable silver and china items.

**39** President Andrew Johnson approved plans to construct a new White House, but Congress did not provide the money.

**40** President Chester A. Arthur didn't like the building and wanted to tear it down when he arrived in the late 1880s.

**41** CONGRESS DENIED HIS REQUEST BUT OFFERED MONEY TO RENOVATE THE HOME.

**42** The whole White House was quarantined for a few days after one of President Benjamin Harrison's grandchildren came down with scarlet fever.

**43** President Grover Cleveland is the only president to have lived at the White House on two separate occasions.

**44** President Cleveland's nanny would bring his daughter Ruth out on the South Lawn, so the public could see her.

**45** The 100th anniversary of the city of Washington in 1900 was marked with a party at the White House.

**46** November 5, 1902, was President Theodore Roosevelt's first day of work in what's now known as the West Wing.

**47** In 1917, President Woodrow Wilson made the White House Executive Office Building a World War I around-the-clock command center.

**48** Suffragettes—people demanding women's right to vote—picketed at the White House gates for two years in an attempt to get President Wilson's attention.

**49** The pressure helped in the successful effort to pass the 19th Amendment, which gave women the right to vote.

**50** In the 1920s, President Calvin Coolidge oversaw the addition to the White House of a sunroom then known as a "sky parlor."

**51** PRESIDENT WARREN G. HARDING'S OVAL OFFICE DESK WAS DRAPED IN A BLACK COVER AFTER HE DIED IN OFFICE IN 1923.

**52** Franklin D. Roosevelt became the first president to name a woman to his Cabinet when he chose Frances Perkins as secretary of labor in 1933.

**53** Crowds of upset Americans swarmed the White House Grounds on December 7, 1941, as word spread of the Japanese bombing of Pearl Harbor.

**54** After the attacks at Pearl Harbor, the Secret Service considered covering the White House skylights with sand and tin for extra security.

**55** On August 14, 1945, President Harry S. Truman announced the end of World War II from the Oval Office.

**56** While President Truman's daughter, Margaret, was practicing her piano, one of its legs fell through the White House floor.

**57** A SURVEY OF THE HOME AT THAT TIME REVEALED THAT THE WHITE HOUSE WAS IN "IMMINENT DANGER OF COLLAPSE."

**58** President Truman went to Congress and requested the funding to rebuild the White House from the inside out.

**59** As a result, the White House interior was completely dismantled, leaving the house as a shell.

**60** The massive renovation was completed in 1952, four years after it began.

**61** In 1961, President John F. Kennedy personally greeted the millionth visitor to the White House for that year.

**62** When he was 16, Bill Clinton met President Kennedy at the White House, inspiring him to go into politics.

**63** First daughter Caroline Kennedy's ballet class used to practice on the South Lawn.

**64** After his 1963 assassination, President Kennedy's flag-draped coffin laid in state in the East Room for a day.

**65** First Lady Jacqueline Kennedy requested that the East Room look just as it did when President Lincoln's casket lay there 98 years before.

**66** President Lyndon B. Johnson was sworn into office on an airplane after the Kennedy assassination.

**67** The Civil Rights Act of 1964 was signed by President Johnson and witnessed by Martin Luther King, Jr., in the East Room.

**68** President Richard M. Nixon made "the most historic telephone call ever" upon calling astronauts on the moon from the White House in 1969.

**69** In 1974, President Nixon became the first—and only—president to resign from office. He made his resignation speech from the Oval Office.

**70** In 1974, President Gerald R. Ford pardoned President Nixon for any illegal activity he may have done in the White House.

**71** PRESIDENT JIMMY CARTER ROUTINELY STARTED HIS WHITE HOUSE WORKING DAY READING A NEWSPAPER.

**72** President Ronald Reagan appointed the first woman to the Supreme Court, Sandra Day O'Connor, in a 1981 Rose Garden ceremony.

**73** In a White House makeover started during the Carter administration, some 40 coats of paint were removed.

**74** The year 2000 was the 200th anniversary of the first occupancy of the White House.

**75** In 2017, Donald J. Trump moved into the White House as the first president elected without prior service in the military or government.

# HISTORY

**1** It cost around **$230,000** to build the original White House—equivalent to **$4,380,000** at today's price of construction.

**2** THE WHITE HOUSE IS VALUED AT AROUND **$300 million today.**

**3** It took THREE YEARS to complete the REBUILDING of the White House following the fire of 1814.

**4** DURING THE 1,222-DAY **RENOVATION** OF THE WHITE HOUSE THAT FINISHED IN 1952, THE **ROOM COUNT DOUBLED TO 132.**

**5** There are 28 WOOD-BURNING FIREPLACES located throughout the White House.

**6** There are **35 BATHROOMS** among the six levels of the White House.

# 25 WHITE HOUSE FACTS AND FIGURES

**7** YOU'LL ALSO FIND 412 doors, 147 windows, 8 staircases, AND 3 elevators IN THE WHITE HOUSE.

**8** THE SOUTH SIDE OF THE WHITE HOUSE IS ABOUT **SIX INCHES (15 CM) TALLER** THAN THE BUILDING'S NORTH SIDE.

**9** The White House requires 570 gallons (2,158 l) of paint to cover its outside surface.

**10** The **annual budget** to run the White House residence—including the cost of heating, lighting, and the staff's salaries—is **$13 million.**

**11** THE WHITE HOUSE'S FIRST TELEPHONE WAS INSTALLED IN 1877. THE PHONE NUMBER? JUST "1."

**12** CURRENTLY, THE U.S. PRESIDENT RECEIVES **a salary of $400,000** PER YEAR. THE FIRST PRESIDENT, GEORGE WASHINGTON, EARNED **$25,000** PER YEAR.

**13** THE WHITE HOUSE RECEIVES MORE THAN **100,000 emails** AND **3,500 phone calls** A DAY.

**14** SOME **65,000 paper letters** ARRIVE AT THE WHITE HOUSE EVERY WEEK. (THE PRESIDENT READS ONLY A FRACTION OF THEM.)

**15** A wealthy businessman is completing a **$20 MILLION HOME IN IRAQ** that looks almost exactly like the White House.

**16** A **6-foot (1.8-m) fence** CURRENTLY SURROUNDS THE WHITE HOUSE, BUT PLANS ARE UNDER WAY TO RAISE IT TO **11 feet (3.4 m).**

**17** THE WHITE HOUSE SITS ON A PLOT AS BIG AS **18 football fields.**

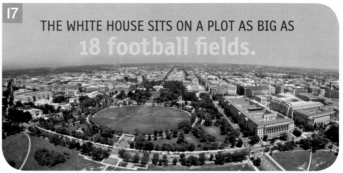

# TO COUNT ON

**18** NEARLY THE SIZE OF A **basketball court,** THE **East Room** IS THE LARGEST ROOM IN THE WHITE HOUSE.

**19** PRESIDENT THEODORE ROOSEVELT ONCE **shook hands** WITH 8,513 PEOPLE AT A WHITE HOUSE FUNCTION—A RECORD FOR A **head of state.**

**20** THERE ARE CLOSE TO **1,900 full-time employees** AT THE WHITE HOUSE, INCLUDING SOME **100** WHO WORK IN THE RESIDENCE.

**21** There are some **2,700 books** written by American authors, or about American history, in the **White House Library.**

**22** EIGHT PRESIDENTS WERE BORN IN **VIRGINIA,** MORE THAN ANY OTHER STATE.

**25** The White House has more than **13 MILLION TWITTER** followers.

**23** As part of a worldwide record-setting effort, 464 students did **JUMPING JACKS** on the White House Lawn in 2011.

**24** A MAN IN TEXAS SPENT **$250,000** TO BUILD A REPLICA OF THE **OVAL OFFICE** IN HIS HOME.

49

# 15 BLOOMING FACTS ABOUT THE

❶ A gardening enthusiast, President Thomas Jefferson **planted** sycamore, poplar, cedar, and oak **trees** around the grounds of the White House.

❷ President James Madison planted what's believed to be the first presidential vegetable garden, complete with cabbage, carrots, broccoli, and more.

❸ **President John Quincy Adams,** who used to garden **early in the morning,** developed the White House's first flower garden.

❹ The large **magnolia tree** beside the South Portico is named for a tree brought to the White House from **Tennessee** by President Andrew Jackson.

❺ President Jackson **planted the tree in honor of his wife, Rachel,** who died just months before he moved into the White House.

❻ In 2006, a 100-year-old elm tree planted by President Theodore Roosevelt in front of the White House toppled over during a summer storm.

❼ In 1913, First Lady Ellen Wilson **planted the first roses** in what is now known as the Rose Garden.

❽ Nearly 50 years later, President John F. Kennedy had the **Rose Garden redesigned** to use it as a venue for **outdoor ceremonies.**

**White House Rose Garden**

50

# WHITE HOUSE GARDENS AND GROUNDS

**9** The **Rose Garden** is the site for **bill signings, press conferences,** and **diplomatic receptions.**

**10** Each year, White House gardeners plant some **3,500 tulip bulbs** to bloom in the **Rose Garden** in the spring.

**11** A White House gardener once **hung baskets of peanuts** on tree trunks to prevent squirrels from **eating tulip bulbs.**

**12** President Jimmy Carter planted pine and maple trees from his family's farm in Georgia around the White House.

**13** Before the arrival of important guests, National Park Service employees once covered up **brown patches** in the White House Lawn with **green spray paint.**

**14** During **World War II,** Diana Hopkins, daughter of a presidential adviser, planted a **"Victory Garden"** on the White House Lawn to supplement the food supply.

**15** In 2016, some 65,000 **honeybees** called the White House gardens home, producing some **225 pounds (102 kg)** of honey in one year.

# 15 ENJOYABLE FACTS ABOUT

1 Skilled **horseback rider** George Washington took **regular rides** on his favorite horse, Nelson.

2 The first **billiards table** was brought into the White House in 1825 by John Quincy Adams, who **challenged his guests to games.**

3 An avid **book collector,** President Thomas Jefferson amassed a collection of 6,487 books that are now in the **Library of Congress.**

4 **Chess** was a favorite activity of President James Madison, who was said to play **four-hour-long games** with friends.

5 **Cat-lover** President Abraham Lincoln had a huge interest in animals, **taking in strays** and spending some of his free time **playing with his pets.**

6 President Ulysses S. Grant had a **creative side** and enjoyed **sketching** and **painting with watercolors.**

7 **Car enthusiast** William Howard Taft considered himself a "motorist" and became the first president to **attend an auto show** in 1910.

8 **Talented musician** Warren G. Harding played the **tuba** to **celebrate his nomination** at the 1920 Democratic Convention.

President John F. Kennedy and First Lady Jacqueline Kennedy (center) go sailing with friends.

# PRESIDENTIAL PASTIMES

**9** President Franklin D. Roosevelt was a **philatelist, or stamp collector.** His collection of some **20,000 stamps** was one of the largest in the country.

**10** President Calvin Coolidge enjoyed **fishing** and spent a summer **away from the White House** in South Dakota so he could **cast lines**.

**11** **Boating** was one of President John F. Kennedy's favorite hobbies. His sailboat *Manitou* was nicknamed the **"Floating White House."**

**12** President Ronald Reagan was a **strong swimmer** who frequently **logged laps** in the White House pool.

**13** President **Jimmy Carter** collected **antique bottles and jars,** the first U.S. president to do so.

**14** President Bill Clinton was crazy for crosswords and once wrote the clues for a puzzle in the *New York Times*.

**15** Golf fan **President Donald J. Trump** has built 17 golf courses around the world and once hit a **hole-in-one** on one of these courses.

**1** George Washington and his wife, Martha, established the **CUSTOM OF WELCOMING GUESTS** to the president's home.

**2** THE *FIRST* FIRST COUPLE **HOSTED DINNERS** FOR MEMBERS OF CONGRESS EVERY THURSDAY AT THEIR HOUSE IN NEW YORK.

**3** PRESIDENT WASHINGTON IS SAID TO HAVE RUDELY **DRUMMED HIS SILVERWARE** ON THE TABLETOP WHILE HIS GUESTS CHATTED.

**4** At his Inauguration in 1829, President Andrew Jackson was nearly **CRUSHED TO DEATH** by a crowd of **20,000** people all wanting to **SHAKE HIS HAND.**

**5** To lure people away from the house, **refreshments** were served outside. They included **ice cream, cake, and lemonade.**

# 25 ENTERTAINING FACTS ABOUT

**6** FIRST LADY **DOLLEY MADISON** WAS FAMOUS FOR HER WEEKLY PARTIES FOR POLITICIANS AND D.C. LOCALS TO **CHAT** AND **LISTEN TO LIVE MUSIC.**

**7** The parties were also known as **CRUSHES** since up to **400 GUESTS** would squeeze together in one room.

**8** Dolley Madison broke tradition by sitting at the **HEAD OF THE TABLE** during her parties, with her husband seated at her side.

**9** On February 5, 1862, First Lady Mary Lincoln hosted a **GRAND RECEPTION** that the *Washington Star* **NEWSPAPER** called the "most superb affair of its kind ever seen."

**10** FIRST LADY JULIA GRANT ADDED **SOPHISTICATED TASTE** TO WHITE HOUSE PARTIES, HOSTING ONE **MEMORABLE DINNER** WITH **29 COURSES.**

**11** President John Tyler hosted a fancy **CHILDREN'S BALL** in honor of his granddaughter, Mary Fairlee, who greeted guests **DRESSED AS A FAIRY.**

**12** FROM 1801 TO 1932, THE WHITE HOUSE HOSTED A **NEW YEAR'S DAY** RECEPTION THAT WAS **OPEN** TO THE **PUBLIC.**

**13** UP TO **6,000 PEOPLE** WOULD WAIT IN A LINE SNAKING AROUND THE BLOCK FOR A CHANCE TO SHAKE THE PRESIDENT'S HAND.

**14** TO CELEBRATE THE END OF PRESIDENT THEODORE ROOSEVELT'S **SECOND TERM,** FIRST LADY EDITH ROOSEVELT THREW A CHILDREN'S PARTY FOR SOME **600 GUESTS.**

**15** At the party, President Roosevelt himself SERVED THE FOOD, which included **600** CREAMED OYSTERS.

**16** During White House celebrations, President Roosevelt's **SIX CHILDREN** would **PEEK** at partygoers from a perch at the top of the **GRAND STAIRCASE.**

**17** President Dwight D. Eisenhower hosted a **WESTERN-THEMED** birthday party for his grandson, David, where the **FAMOUS COWBOY** Roy Rogers made a surprise appearance.

# WHITE HOUSE PARTIES

**18** When first daughter CAROLINE KENNEDY crashed a White House party in her nightgown, the Marine Band played a CHILDREN'S SONG for her.

**19** President Lyndon B. Johnson hosted a **CHRISTMAS PARTY** in the East Room for children. The party was organized by his younger daughter, **LUCI BAINES JOHNSON.**

**20** Guests of a 1978 **Halloween party** hosted by Jimmy Carter were welcomed by a 16-foot (4.9-m) plywood **jack-o'-lantern** at the White House's **entrance.**

**21** In 1981, President Ronald Reagan's surprise 70th birthday party featured dancing, a **LOBSTER** and **VEAL** dinner, and a **DOZEN CAKES.**

**22** BILL AND HILLARY CLINTON DRESSED UP AS JAMES AND DOLLEY MADISON AT A BIRTHDAY AND HALLOWEEN PARTY FOR THE FIRST LADY IN 1993.

**23** President George W. Bush established the tradition of the annual White House **Hanukkah party** in 2001.

**24** THE WHITE HOUSE HOSTED A "MAD HATTER" COSTUME BALL IN 2009, TRANSFORMING THE STATE DINING ROOM INTO ALICE'S WONDERLAND.

**25** THE COSTUME BALL—FOR CHILDREN OF ACTIVE MILITARY—WAS COMPLETE WITH ENORMOUS STUFFED ANIMALS IN CHAIRS, BONE-SHAPED COOKIES, AND FRUIT PUNCH SERVED IN BLOOD VIALS.

**1** Every year, on the day after Easter, more than 35,000 KIDS and their parents hit the White House Lawn for the EASTER EGG ROLL.

**2** Participants each push a HARD-BOILED EGG across the lawn with a large KITCHEN SPOON. The first one across the line wins!

**3** PRESIDENT ANDREW JOHNSON'S GRANDCHILDREN first rolled dyed eggs on the CAPITOL GROUNDS in the mid-1800s.

**4** The event caught on and soon many families began heading to the LAWNS OF CAPITOL HILL to picnic and roll eggs.

**5** In the 1870s, Congress passed a law BANNING EGG ROLLS on the Capitol lawn after complaints that it TORE UP THE GRASS.

**11** The modern-day EASTER EGG ROLL RACES were introduced in 1974, with kids using spoons from the White House KITCHEN.

**12** MUSIC was first added to the party in 1889, with the United States Marine Band playing on the lawn.

**13** Today, POP STARS like Justin Bieber have PERFORMED ON THE SOUTH LAWN during the Easter Egg Roll.

**14** First Lady Grace Coolidge brought her PET RACCOON, Rebecca, to the 1927 egg roll.

**15** Other highlights of the Easter Egg Roll have included a PETTING ZOO, a CIRCUS, and GIANT BALLOONS to play with.

**21** The EASTER BUNNY made its first appearance at the egg roll in 1969.

**22** Since then, other characters, such as COOKIE MONSTER, have strolled the White House lawns during the event.

**23** President Jimmy Carter trotted out a 1,200-POUND (544-KG) COW named BIG RED to the 1977 roll.

**24** In 1981, President Ronald Reagan and First Lady Nancy Reagan held the first HUNT FOR WOODEN EGGS signed by celebrities.

**25** Wooden eggs have been the OFFICIAL SOUVENIR of the roll ever since.

**31** Only children ages 13 AND YOUNGER—and their parents—CAN PARTICIPATE in the egg roll.

**32** Today, the Easter Egg Roll is the LARGEST ANNUAL EVENT at the White House.

**33** FIRST LADIES Betty Ford and Rosalynn Carter both passed out PLASTIC EGGS WITH NOTES INSIDE to all participants.

# 35 SPOONFUL FACTS ABOUT THE

**6** Around 1878, President Rutherford B. Hayes INVITED THE PUBLIC to roll their eggs at the WHITE HOUSE instead.

**7** In 1885, President Grover Cleveland GREETED EGG ROLLERS in the East Room.

**8** President Cleveland let his DOG HECTOR RUN AROUND on the South Lawn during the egg roll.

**9** In the late 1800s, kids didn't just roll eggs, they also PLAYED GAMES that involved hard-boiled eggs being CRACKED OPEN.

**10** The smell from all of the eggs cracked during these games produced an odor some said could be SNIFFED OUT FROM MILES AWAY.

**16** In 1917, the egg roll was moved from the WHITE HOUSE GROUNDS to the lawn surrounding the WASHINGTON MONUMENT.

**17** In 1921, a massive crowd of more than 50,000 CHILDREN showed up to roll their eggs.

**18** That year, President Warren G. Harding brought out his BELOVED DOG, LADDIE BOY, to meet the kids.

**19** The egg roll was CANCELLED during the TWO WORLD WARS and during the White House RENOVATION from 1948 to 1952.

**20** In 1929, the Easter Egg Roll was BROADCAST ON THE RADIO for the first time, showcasing music by THE MARINE BAND.

**26** Today, tickets are available only through an ONLINE LOTTERY so that kids from ALL OVER THE COUNTRY can attend.

**27** Each year, some 300,000 people ENTER THE LOTTERY for just around 35,000 AVAILABLE TICKETS.

**28** TICKET-HOLDERS get a TWO-HOUR TIME SLOT to play and roll before they're ushered out and the next group is brought in.

**29** In the days leading up to the event, about 14,500 EGGS are cooked and dyed in the White House kitchen.

**30** Some 1,200 VOLUNTEERS help to pull off the Easter Egg Roll every year.

**34** President and Mrs. Obama's signatures, and paw prints of FIRST DOGS BO AND SUNNY OBAMA, decorated recent souvenir eggs.

**35** A good-for-your-teeth LOLLIPOP—invented by a SEVEN-YEAR-OLD— was served at the 2016 Easter Egg Roll.

# EASTER EGG ROLL

# 15 WHIZZ FACTS ABOUT

**❶** The Inauguration of President James K. Polk was the first presidential swearing in to be reported by telegraph.

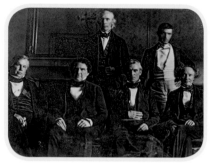

**❷** A shot of President Polk and his Cabinet, taken in the 1840s, is among the **first photos of the inside of the White House.**

**❸** In 1889, Benjamin Harrison **recorded a 30-second message**—making him the first president to have his **voice preserved.**

**❹** President Grover Cleveland answered his Oval Office phone personally.

**❺** The government began using an **early computer** while President Franklin D. Roosevelt was in office in the **1940s.**

**❻** In 1955, **Dwight D. Eisenhower** became the first president to appear on **color television.**

OFFICE OF THE JOINT CHIEFS OF STAFF

**7** President John F. Kennedy established a hotline between the **United States** and **the Soviet Union** to speed up **communication between the countries.**

**❽** President Jimmy Carter had personal **computers and printers** installed in the White House in 1978.

GREEN

**The Situation Room is the hub of the White House communications system.**

# GADGETS IN THE WHITE HOUSE

**9** George H. W. Bush sent the **first email as a president in office** in 1992.

**10** One of the **two emails** that President Bill Clinton reportedly sent during his administration was to an **orbiting space shuttle.**

**11** White House Easter Egg Roll festivities were **broadcast live on the Internet** for the first time in 1998.

**12** **George W. Bush** was the first president to own both an **iPod** and a **Segway** while in office.

**13** In his first ever **Instagram post** in 2014, Vice President Joe Biden **posted a selfie** with President Barack Obama.

**14** In 2016, the White House posted its **first picture on the Snapchat app,** a shot of the **Oval Office.**

**15** There are more than **80 official White House Twitter** accounts.

**1** For decades, presidents and their families have **pardoned a turkey** before each Thanksgiving.

**2** The presidential pardon **saves the bird** from being served on **Thanksgiving**.

**3** President Jimmy Carter lit the first **National Menorah** in 1979, a tradition that lives on today.

**4** President George Washington established the tradition of delivering a **farewell address** to the public upon **leaving office**.

**5** Today, it remains customary for a president to **deliver a final address** on television from the White House.

**6** Before a new president moves into the White House, the **current first lady** invites the spouse of the president-elect to **tour the private quarters**.

**7** For many administrations, the outgoing president has **left a note** to the new leader in the **Oval Office**.

**8** On **Memorial Day** each May, the president or vice president lays a wreath at the **Tomb of the Unknown Soldier** in Arlington, Virginia.

**President Barack Obama pardons a turkey during a White House Thanksgiving ceremony.**

# WHITE HOUSE RITUALS

**9** It's tradition for the president to call and **congratulate the winners of the Super Bowl** after the big game.

**10** The president also welcomes **collegiate champions** and **winning sports teams** to the White House for **special ceremonies**.

**11** Since 2009, the president has lit a **diya**, or **oil lamp**, in the White House each autumn to celebrate **Diwali**, a Hindu festival of lights.

**12** A tradition that began in 1920, the annual White House Correspondents' dinner honors reporters who cover the White House.

**13** It's also become customary for the president to address the guests at the correspondents' dinner with a lighthearted, funny speech.

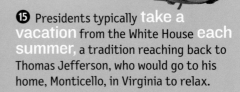

**14** The president typically throws out the first pitch on opening day for the Washington Nationals baseball team—a tradition that began more than 100 years ago.

**15** Presidents typically take a vacation from the White House each summer, a tradition reaching back to Thomas Jefferson, who would go to his home, Monticello, in Virginia to relax.

# 15 TRENDY FACTS ABOUT

**1** President George Washington liked to outfit his **horses** in **leopard-skin robes.**

**2** Partial to **old, beat-up clothes and hats,** President Zachary Taylor was sometimes **mistaken for a farmer.**

**3** The pink gown Mamie Eisenhower wore to the 1953 Inaugural Balls **sparkled** with more than **2,000 rhinestones.**

**4** First Lady Helen "Nellie" Taft donated her **bejeweled Inaugural gown** from 1909 to the National Museum of American History, where it can still **be seen today.**

**5** The **White House wait staff** always wear **tuxedos** to serve formal dinners.

**6** Thomas Jefferson was known to **greet dignitaries** while wearing **a robe and slippers.**

**7** To fight off the chill at his 1909 Inauguration, President William Howard Taft wore a **fur-lined overcoat with a fur collar and cuffs.**

**8** First Lady Jacqueline Kennedy was considered a **fashion icon** in the 1960s, with American women everywhere going for the **"Jackie Look."**

First Lady Johnson and three models at the 1968 White House fashion show

# WHITE HOUSE FASHION

**9** The White House hosted its first fashion show in 1968, with models strutting down a runway set up in the State Dining Room.

**10** Fashionable First Lady Edith Wilson preferred French clothing and took shopping trips to Paris in the early 1900s.

**11** First Lady Pat Nixon is said to be the first wife of a president to wear pants in public while living at the White House.

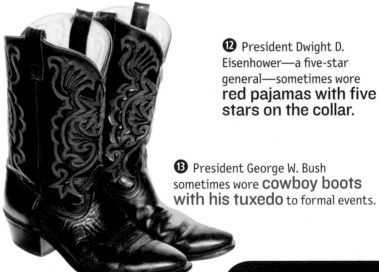

**12** President Dwight D. Eisenhower—a five-star general—sometimes wore **red pajamas with five stars on the collar.**

**13** President George W. Bush sometimes wore **cowboy boots with his tuxedo** to formal events.

**14** Dolley Madison—a fashionable first lady—was known for her **signature turban,** which she often **accented with a feather.**

**15** It took **100 hours** for a team of three women to **hand-bead** First Lady Laura Bush's first Inaugural gown, which she wore in 2001.

# 15 SPORTY FACTS ABOUT

**1** The White House Grounds feature a **tennis court**, a **putting green**, and a **swimming pool**.

**2** The swimming pool, built in 1975 by President Gerald R. Ford, features a **diving board** and a **spacious cabana**.

**3** President Harry S. Truman installed the first **horseshoe pitch** just off the Oval Office. It was later removed.

**4** In 1989, **President George H. W. Bush** added a new horseshoe pitch and would challenge world **leaders** to a toss.

**5** President Harry S. Truman officially opened the first **White House bowling alley** in 1947.

**6** Some 22 years later, President Richard M. Nixon had a new one-lane **bowling alley** built below the driveway leading to the White House's **North Portico**.

**7** The first White House **putting green** was installed by President Dwight D. Eisenhower in 1954.

**8** A **jogging track** around the driveway of the **south grounds** was built during President Bill Clinton's first term.

President Ronald Reagan tests out his new golf putter on a White House carpet.

# THE WHITE HOUSE

**9** President **George H. W. Bush** invited **tennis champions** to play with him on the White House courts.

**10** President Barack Obama added **removable basketball hoops** to the tennis court so he could practice **shooting hoops.**

**11** President Thomas Jefferson regularly **rode his horse** from the White House through the woods of D.C. for up to **two hours every day.**

**12** President Theodore Roosevelt worked on his fitness while in office by **lifting weights** and **practicing jujitsu.**

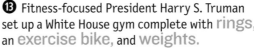

**13** Fitness-focused President Harry S. Truman set up a White House gym complete with **rings**, an **exercise bike**, and **weights.**

**14** President William Henry Harrison **walked for miles every day** and would often be spotted **strolling** to the Washington Monument or on the streets of D.C.

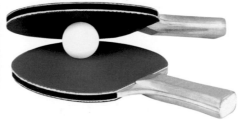

**15** There's a game room with **billiard** and **Ping-Pong** tables on the third floor of the White House.

**1**
THOMAS JEFFERSON was the first president to greet others with a HANDSHAKE instead of a BOW.

**2**
MILLARD FILLMORE was the first president to have a BATHTUB WITH RUNNING WATER in the White House.

**3**
PRESIDENT JAMES MONROE was the first president to travel on a STEAMSHIP while in office.

**8**
JIMMY CARTER was the first president to be BORN IN A HOSPITAL.

**9**
BARACK OBAMA was the first AFRICAN AMERICAN to serve as U.S. PRESIDENT.

**10**
RUTHERFORD B. HAYES was the first president to VISIT THE WEST COAST while in office.

**15**
JOHN F. KENNEDY was the first president to be born in the 20TH CENTURY.

**16**
President Kennedy's son, John F. Kennedy, Jr., was the FIRST INFANT to be raised in the White House since the EARLY 1900s.

**17**
In 1967, President LYNDON B. JOHNSON appointed Thurgood Marshall as the first ever AFRICAN AMERICAN to the SUPREME COURT.

**18**
AIR FORCE ONE touched down in HAVANA, CUBA, for the first time in 2016.

**22**
In 2014, the first ever White House STUDENT FILM FESTIVAL honored YOUNG FILMMAKERS from across the country.

**23**
CALVIN COOLIDGE was the first president to be featured on a coin while he was STILL LIVING.

**24**
In 2001, PRESIDENT BILL CLINTON became the first president to be MARRIED TO A U.S. SENATOR.

**25**
Just days before Bill Clinton left office, First Lady HILLARY CLINTON was sworn in as a NEW YORK SENATOR.

**29**
LYNDON B. JOHNSON was the first president to FLY AROUND THE WORLD visiting other governments.

**30**
President ULYSSES S. GRANT signed the bill establishing YELLOWSTONE NATIONAL PARK as the first national park.

**31**
In 1801, President THOMAS JEFFERSON hosted the first ever White House FOURTH OF JULY celebration.

# 35 FASCINATING

**4** JOHN QUINCY ADAMS is the only president to serve in the HOUSE OF REPRESENTATIVES after his administration.

**5** MARTIN VAN BUREN was the first president to be born an AMERICAN CITIZEN. The rest had been born as BRITISH SUBJECTS.

**6** WILLIAM HENRY HARRISON was the first president to DIE IN OFFICE, after just 32 days in the White House.

**7** Native to KENTUCKY, ABRAHAM LINCOLN was the first president born outside the 13 ORIGINAL STATES.

**11** When he visited PANAMA in 1906, THEODORE ROOSEVELT became the first president in office to TRAVEL OVERSEAS.

**12** Theodore Roosevelt was the first president to win the NOBEL PEACE PRIZE, in 1906.

**13** DWIGHT D. EISENHOWER was the first president to be legally prohibited from seeking a THIRD TERM.

**14** WILLIAM HOWARD TAFT was the first president to throw out the first pitch of a PROFESSIONAL BASEBALL GAME.

**19** JOHN QUINCY ADAMS was the first president to PLANT ORNAMENTAL TREES around the White House.

**20** PRESIDENT OBAMA was the first president to RECEIVE MESSAGES on FACEBOOK.

**21** President WARREN G. HARDING had the first RADIO installed in the White House, in 1922.

**26** In 1961, Dr. Janet Travell became the first ever FEMALE WHITE HOUSE PHYSICIAN, tending to Presidents Kennedy and Johnson.

**27** JOHN QUINCY ADAMS was the first president to have his PHOTO TAKEN—although it was snapped after he left the White House.

**28** WALTER MONDALE, who served with Jimmy Carter, was the FIRST VICE PRESIDENT to have an OFFICE in the WHITE HOUSE.

**32** HERBERT HOOVER was the first president to be born WEST OF THE MISSISSIPPI RIVER.

**33** ROSALYNN CARTER set up the first Office of the First Lady in the EAST WING in 1977.

**34** In 2015, the White House hosted its first Demo Day showcasing BUSINESS IDEAS and projects from ENTREPRENEURS.

**35** The White House posted its first VIRTUAL REALITY VIDEO in 2016, featuring a look at Yosemite National Park.

**Fourth of July fireworks display over the Washington Monument and Lincoln Memorial**

# FIRSTS AT THE WHITE HOUSE

67

# 15 BLAZING FACTS ABOUT

**1** From 1812 to 1814, the United States **waged war with Great Britain** over freedom of the seas.

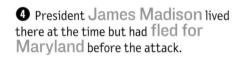

**2** During the summer of 1814, the capital city of **Washington, D.C.,** emerged as the **center of the War of 1812.**

**3** On August 23, 1814, British troops **seized control of Washington** and set the **White House ablaze.**

**4** President **James Madison** lived there at the time but had **fled for Maryland** before the attack.

**5** President Madison sent a message to his wife, **Dolley,** to leave the White House—which she managed to do **successfully.**

**6** Among items that First Lady Madison packed up before leaving the house were **silverware,** her **caged parrot,** and a now famous portrait of George Washington.

**7** About 150 British troops marched down **Pennsylvania Avenue** and **barged into the White House.**

British military forces burn Washington, D.C., in 1814.

**8** The British troops reportedly feasted on the **president's dinner,** which had been set on the table **before the first lady fled.**

# THE FIRE OF 1814

**9** The British troops sparked the raging fire by **hurling torches through the windows** to ignite the White House furniture.

**10** Before they set the fire, the soldiers **looted the White House**, snatching souvenirs like **President Madison's medicine chest.**

**11** The inferno from the White House and other nearby burning buildings burned so bright that it could be seen from about 50 miles (80 km) away.

**12** A **summer thunderstorm** put out the fire, leaving a **charred and badly damaged** White House.

**13** Six months later, the **war ended in a stalemate,** with **the United States and Great Britain** agreeing to keep things as they were before the battle.

**14** You can still see some scorch marks from the fire on unpainted stones near an old entrance to the mansion beneath the North Portico.

**15** The house—then known as the **Executive Mansion**—was soon rebuilt and **repainted white to cover the smoke marks.** People began calling it the White House.

# 15 SWEET FACTS ABOUT

**1** The White House's **executive pastry chef** oversees the dessert menus for all **social events** at the White House.

**2** Traditionally, the president and first lady hand out **candy** to local children who visit the White House on **Halloween.**

**3** Over the holidays, the State Dining Room often features a **massive gingerbread or chocolate model of the White House** that can take nearly a **year** to plan and create.

**4** Past gingerbread houses have often been **wired with lighting** to illuminate their **tiny individual rooms.**

**5** President Thomas Jefferson had an **ice house built** on the White House Grounds so that he could have **ice cream all year long.**

**6** While Jefferson was the first president to have ice cream in the White House, **Dolley Madison** later made it **famous** at the house **by regularly serving it at her dinner parties.**

**7** First Lady Madison plucked **small, sweet oysters** from the Potomac River to create her **favorite ice cream flavor—oyster.**

# WHITE HOUSE TREATS

**8** President Franklin D. Roosevelt once received a 110-pound (50-kg) **fruitcake**, complete with **mountains and trees made of sugar.**

**9** At Abraham Lincoln's **Inaugural Ball** in 1865, guests feasted on **pyramids of pastries and macaroons.**

**10** **"Flowerpot sundaes"**—layers of sponge cake, ice cream, and meringue, topped with a fresh flower—were served at first daughter Luci Baines Johnson's **White House engagement party.**

**11** A fan of French cuisine, First Lady Jacqueline Kennedy served desserts like chocolate mousse and crème brûlée to White House guests.

**12** When the president of Mexico visited the White House in 1984, the pastry chef crafted kiwi sorbet cactuses with sugar spines as a nod to the special guest.

**13** Sweet-toothed **President Ronald Reagan** was known to **sneak desserts** when his wife, Nancy, wasn't around.

**14** Allergic to chocolate, President **Bill Clinton** safely satisfied his sweet tooth with **carrot cake.**

**15** First Lady **Mamie Eisenhower's** famed **"Million Dollar Fudge"** recipe is still popular some 60 years after she left the White House.

**fishing boat dessert created by a White House pastry chef**

71

# ⑮ FACTS ABOUT

**1** To get away from it all, presidents can head to **Camp David**, a **mountain retreat** about 60 miles (97 km) from the White House.

**❷** Built in 1942, Camp David features a swimming pool, a skeet-shooting range, and a bowling alley.

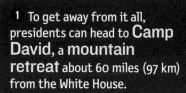

**❸** To get to Camp David—or any other nearby location—the president lifts off on **Marine One**, the official **White House helicopter**.

**❹** For longer trips, the president flies on **Air Force One**, which is equipped with a **bedroom, 19 TVs,** and a **gym.**

**❺** Because surrounding airspace is cleared for Air Force One, **the president never has to wait** on a delayed flight and can leave—and land—anytime.

**❻** A White House pastry maker is always available to whip up **elaborate cakes** for special occasions, like **birthday parties.**

**❼** For her 16th birthday, Chelsea Clinton received a cake decorated with a picture of a Washington, D.C., **driver's license** and a **car made out of sugar.**

Marine One with the president on board lands on the South Lawn of the White House.

# PRESIDENTIAL PERKS

**8** Once a day, the White House cafeteria—also known as the Mess—serves free french fries to all West Wing employees.

**9** On Fridays, the Mess offers free frozen yogurt—and toppings.

**10** The president not only makes $400,000 a year but also receives another $50,000 for expenses and $100,000 for travel.

**11** Former U.S. presidents receive an annual salary of around $200,000, plus a paid staff and office space.

**12** The White House fridges and pantries are stocked with free drinks and snacks for staff.

**13** Friends and family can send letters directly to the president and first lady using a top secret personal zip code.

**14** To help his golf game, President Barack Obama had a virtual driving range set up in the White House.

**15** Guests to the White House can munch on M&M's in boxes with the presidential seal on them.

**1** There are some **15 monuments, memorials, and statues** in President's Park—the land **surrounding the White House.**

BUILT IN 1853, A STATUE OF PRESIDENT ANDREW JACKSON ON A HORSE NEAR THE WHITE HOUSE WAS THE FIRST EQUESTRIAN STATUE IN THE WORLD TO BE BALANCED SOLELY ON THE **HORSE'S HIND LEGS.**

**3** The entire statue was cast in a total of **10 pieces**—four of the horse and six of President Jackson— weighing a total of 15 tons (13.6 t).

**4** There are REPLICAS OF THE STATUE in New Orleans, Louisiana; Nashville, Tennessee; and Jacksonville, Florida.

**5** THE PRESIDENT JACKSON STATUE—AND **four other memorials**—ARE ALL PART OF A **166-year-old garden** JUST NORTH OF THE WHITE HOUSE.

# 25 HARD FACTS ABOUT WHITE

**6** The garden's statues **align** with the **setting sun** on the summer and winter **solstices,** occurring in June and December each year.

**7** THERE'S A STATUE HONORING THE **Boy Scouts of America** JUST SOUTH OF THE WHITE HOUSE, ON THE **Ellipse.**

**8** **Boy Scout troops from around the country collected dimes** to raise enough money to build the bronze statue, which was unveiled in **1964.**

**9** A bust of President **George Washington,** created in the **1790s,** is said to be worth **$50,000.**

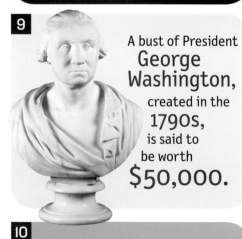

**12** A fountain and sculpture on the Ellipse serve as a memorial for **two Americans who died** aboard the R.M.S. *Titanic.*

**10** The Washington bust, as well as one of ABRAHAM LINCOLN, can be found in small niches—or ALCOVES—along the White House's CROSS HALL.

**11** SOME OF THE **WHITE HOUSE'S** MARBLE BUSTS OF PRESIDENTS LIKE JOHN ADAMS AND JAMES MADISON DATE BACK **225 YEARS.**

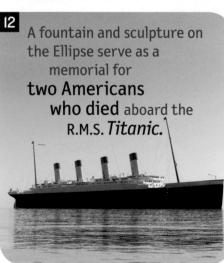

**13** The Zero Milestone—a rectangular monument on the Ellipse—was originally meant to mark the beginning of **all roadways** in the United States.

**14** The **granite marker** has stood in front of the White House since 1923, although it's no longer **a central point** for the country's **highways.**

**15**
Franklin D. Roosevelt's dog, Fala—a **presidential pet** at the White House—is now memorialized in a **statue on the National Mall.**

**16** A 183-year-old statue of **THOMAS JEFFERSON,** now in the **U.S. CAPITOL BUILDING,** once stood on the grounds of the White House.

**17** THE JEFFERSON STATUE WAS MOVED IN 1873 TO MAKE ROOM ON THE NORTH LAWN FOR A **fountain,** NEW WALKWAYS, AND **flower beds** IN THE SHAPE OF A **pinwheel.**

# HOUSE STATUES AND BUSTS

**18** A SMALL BUST OF U.S. FOUNDING FATHER **BENJAMIN FRANKLIN**—MADE BY A FRENCH SCULPTOR IN 1810—SITS ON A TABLE IN THE **GREEN ROOM.**

**19** Hundred-year-old busts of famed explorers **AMERIGO VESPUCCI** and **CHRISTOPHER COLUMBUS** can be spotted in the **WHITE HOUSE'S BLUE ROOM.**

**20** AS FIRST LADY, HILLARY CLINTON CREATED AN OUTDOOR **sculpture garden** ON THE WHITE HOUSE GROUNDS, SHOWCASING WORKS OF **American artists.**

**21** Artists used **3-D printing technology** to build a **full-scale model** of President Barack Obama's head.

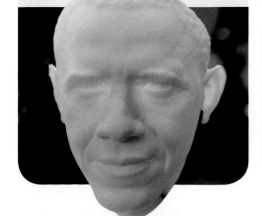

**22** A bust of Winston Churchill has been in the White House since the 1960s.

**23** Gilbert Stuart, the artist who painted the **FAMOUS GEORGE WASHINGTON PORTRAIT,** also created two **BUSTS** of the first president.

**25** ABRAHAM LINCOLN ONCE POSED FOR A TEENAGE SCULPTOR, WHO CREATED A FULL-LENGTH STATUE OF THE PRESIDENT THAT'S NOW IN THE U.S. CAPITOL.

**24** President Bill Clinton had **BUSTS OF ABRAHAM LINCOLN** and **FRANKLIN D. ROOSEVELT** serve as **BOOKENDS** on the table behind his desk in the Oval Office.

# 15 COVERT FACTS ABOUT POLICE SECRET SERVICE

**1** In the early years of the White House, the **president roamed freely** in the mansion and its grounds without a security team to **protect him** or **the home.**

**2** **President Abraham Lincoln** established the **U.S. Secret Service** on April 14, 1865. Its first official day of service was July 5, 1865.

**3** Originally part of the **Treasury Department,** the Secret Service was created to **crack down on counterfeit money.**

**4** President Franklin Pierce, who had a **round-the-clock bodyguard,** never left the White House by himself—a tradition that **continues today.**

**5** In 1902, after the assassination of President William McKinley, **full-time agents** were **assigned to guard the White House.**

**6** Today, there are more than **3,000** **Secret Service** agents working around the world, including **1,300 offering protection to the White House.**

**7** Agents also **guard the vice president,** their **families,** and **former presidents** and **first ladies.**

**8** A highly trained Secret Service agent **chauffeurs the presidential limousine,** which is able to launch **tear gas** if under attack.

# WHITE HOUSE SECURITY

**9** U.S. Secret Service agents use **code names** for **presidents and first ladies**, like "Rawhide" and "Rainbow" for Ronald and Nancy Reagan, and "Trailblazer" for George W. Bush.

**10** In 2015, a **four-year-old child** climbed under a temporary barrier in front of the White House fence, causing the Secret Service to **shut down the mansion** for a few moments.

**11** The **fence surrounding the White House** is topped with **supersharp steel spikes** to keep intruders out.

**12** The Secret Service is making plans to build an **exact replica of the White House** for security training.

**13** On official journeys, Secret Service **close protection vehicles** are fitted with the U.S. flag and presidential seals.

**14** Secret Service agents must go through **several months** of **specialized training**, including **first aid, criminal law,** and **psychology.**

**15** In 1978, an agent **rescued first daughter** Amy Carter from the **path** of a **charging circus elephant.**

A member of the U.S. Secret Service and a police dog patrol in front of the White House.

**1** A reference to the "First Lady" was first printed in a magazine on March 31, 1860.

**2** IN THE EARLY YEARS, THE PRESIDENT'S WIFE WAS OFTEN CALLED "THE LADY OF THE WHITE HOUSE."

**3** Other terms, like "Mrs. President" and "Presidentress" were also used early on.

**4** The term "first lady" likely started with President Rutherford B. Hayes's wife, Lucy, in the 1870s.

**5** Several widowed presidents, including Thomas Jefferson and Martin Van Buren, had family and friends step in to fill the first lady role.

**6** James Buchanan, the only bachelor president, had his niece Harriet Lane serve as first lady.

**7** Martha Washington was the first first lady to appear on a U.S. postage stamp, in 1902.

**8** Elizabeth Monroe and her husband, James, spoke mostly French in the White House.

**9** At five feet two inches (157 cm), Mary Lincoln stood more than a foot (30 cm) shorter than her husband.

**10** Lucy Hayes was the first first lady to hold a college degree, having graduated from Wesleyan Female College in Cincinnati, Ohio.

**11** Pat Nixon was the first first lady with a graduate degree—a master's from the University of Southern California.

**12** Ellen Wilson, first wife of Woodrow, was a professional artist and had a painting studio in the White House.

**13** First Lady Louisa Adams once hosted a ball for General Andrew Jackson, who went on to defeat her husband in the presidential race four years later.

**14** President Wilson's second wife, Edith, was one of the few women in Washington, D.C., with her own car and often drove around town.

**15** Edith Wilson earned the nickname of "First Lady President" after her husband fell ill and she took over many of his duties and decisions as president.

**16** Bess Truman never gave a single interview during her time in the White House.

**17** Edith Roosevelt made history when she became the first first lady to travel overseas with her husband, Theodore.

**18** FIRST LADY EDITH ROOSEVELT WAS THE FIRST TO DISPLAY PRESIDENTIAL CHINA AT THE WHITE HOUSE— NOW A PERMANENT EXHIBIT IN THE HOME.

**19** Julia Grant's autobiography, published 70 years after her death in 1902, was the first printed memoir of a first lady.

**20** First Lady Melania Trump speaks five languages— Slovenian, English, French, Serbian, and German.

**21** FIRST LADY GRACE COOLIDGE CARED FOR MANY PETS, INCLUDING DUCKLINGS SHE BATHED IN A WHITE HOUSE TUB.

**22** After her husband James's death, First Lady Dolley Madison was so poor she had to take handouts from neighbors.

**23** In 1845, Dolley Madison was selected to be the first private citizen to send a message via telegraph.

**24** A married mother of four, President Chester A. Arthur's sister Mary "Molly" McElroy stepped in as his first lady after his wife died.

**25** Despite serving from 1883 to 1885 and hosting extravagant state dinners, McElroy was never officially recognized as the first lady.

**26** There is no known portrait from life of Thomas Jefferson's wife, Martha, who died 18 years before his election to the presidency.

**27** Four first ladies have lost their husbands in presidential assassinations: Mary Lincoln, Lucretia Garfield, Ida McKinley, and Jacqueline Kennedy.

**28** Barbara Bush, wife of President George H. W. Bush, wrote the best-selling *Millie's Book* about her dog's view of the White House.

**29** During her time in the White House, Lady Bird Johnson, wife of President Lyndon B. Johnson, raised funds to plant trees and flowers in inner-city neighborhoods of Washington, D.C.

**30** Michelle Obama, the first African-American first lady in U.S. history, was also the first to tweet.

**31** Florence Harding took to the skies in a Navy seaplane in 1920, becoming the first presidential spouse to fly.

**32** Lou Hoover served as national president of the Girl Scouts of America before her husband won the presidency.

**33** First Lady Hoover also spoke fluent Chinese.

**34** IDA McKINLEY BANNED ALL THINGS YELLOW FROM THE WHITE HOUSE—EVEN FLOWERS GROWING IN THE GARDEN.

**35** Anna Harrison—briefly first lady—never lived in the White House. Her husband, William Henry, died before she moved in.

**36** The youngest first lady at 21, Frances Cleveland both married and had a baby in the White House.

**37** First Lady Cleveland hosted weekly White House receptions on Saturdays for working women.

**Jefferson Memorial seen through cherry blossoms**

75 FABULOUS FACTS ABOUT

**38** Prior to her time in the White House, Nancy Reagan acted on Broadway and had roles in several movies.

**39** Letitia Tyler was the first president's wife to pass away in the White House when she died in 1842.

**40** John Tyler's second wife, Julia, once requested that the song "Hail to the Chief" play when the president entered a room—a tradition that continues.

**41** First Lady Julia Tyler is believed to be the first president's wife to be photographed.

**42** The photo of Julia Tyler—taken in 1844—was discovered in 1987 and published for the first time in 1990.

**43** Caroline Harrison, wife of President Benjamin Harrison, raised funds for a medical school—only after it agreed to admit women.

**44 FIRST LADY HARRISON OVERSAW THE INSTALLATION OF ELECTRICITY IN THE WHITE HOUSE.**

**45** Mamie Eisenhower reportedly stayed in bed and worked until noon, with her breakfast arriving at 10:30 a.m.

**46** Nellie Taft refused to let butlers with bald heads or mustaches serve in the White House dining room.

**47** In 1909, Nellie Taft rode alongside her husband, William Howard, during his Inaugural Parade—a tradition remaining today.

**48** Jacqueline Kennedy won an Emmy Award for her televised tour of the White House.

**49** A recluse who spent most of her days inside her bedroom, Jane Pierce was known as the "shadow of the White House."

**50** Ida McKinley crocheted hundreds of pairs of slippers during her time in the White House, which she gave away to charity.

**51** Wanting to clean up the Tidal Basin near the White House, Nellie Taft asked for trees to be planted in the area.

**52 JAPAN SENT 3,000 CHERRY TREES TO THE TAFTS, WHICH SOON BECAME FAMOUS FOR THEIR PINK PETALS THAT BLOOM EACH SPRING.**

**53** First Lady Pat Nixon created tours of the White House for the blind and deaf.

**54** Pat Nixon welcomed a pair of pandas to Washington, D.C., after China donated the animals to the National Zoo.

**55** Eliza Johnson helped her husband, Andrew, perfect his reading and writing skills before he was elected president.

**56** First Lady Sarah Polk was so strict, she did not allow any dancing or card playing in the White House.

**57 SARAH POLK ALWAYS EDITED HER HUSBAND JAMES'S SPEECHES.**

**58** Abigail Adams offered advice to her husband, John, as he worked on the Declaration of Independence.

**59** First Lady Abigail Adams was often referred to as "Mrs. President" because of her political knowledge and influence on her husband.

**60** Eleanor Roosevelt, wife of President Franklin D. Roosevelt, wrote a daily newspaper column called "My Day."

**61** In the column, First Lady Roosevelt touched on politics, current events, and things going on in her life.

**62** Louisa Adams, wife of John Quincy Adams, and Melania Trump are the only first ladies born in a foreign country.

**63** Grace Coolidge was a regular in the stands at Washington Senators' baseball games.

**64** In 1933, Eleanor Roosevelt left a White House dinner party to fly around Baltimore with Amelia Earhart.

**65** On a visit to New York in 1807, First Lady Abigail Adams chased down a kidnapper who tried to steal her baby son.

**66** Julia Tyler hosted dances in the White House and is said to have popularized the polka in Washington, D.C.

**67** Elizabeth "Betty" Ford worked as a fashion model and dancer in New York City before marrying her husband, Gerald.

**68** Laura Bush—who started the National Book Festival at the Library of Congress in 2001—was once a school librarian.

**69 FIRST LADY LAURA BUSH IS THE ONLY PRESIDENTIAL WIFE TO BE THE MOTHER OF TWINS.**

**70** First Lady Nixon once called her role the "hardest unpaid job in the world."

**71** Hillary Clinton is the only first lady to hold a political office.

**72** Hillary Clinton is also the only first lady to run for president herself.

**73** Abigail Adams and Barbara Bush are the only first ladies to have both a husband and a son serve as president.

**74** Rosalynn Carter—who often sat in on Cabinet meetings with her husband—was once referred to as the "second most powerful person in the United States."

**75** Michelle Obama's Secret Service code name was "Renaissance."

# FIRST LADIES

**1** There have been 17 documented White House weddings—one for a sitting president, nine for presidential children, and seven for presidents' relatives and close friends.

**2** THE FIRST WEDDING TO TAKE PLACE AT THE WHITE HOUSE WAS FOR **Dolley Madison's sister** LUCY PAYNE WASHINGTON TO THOMAS TODD, IN 1812.

**3** YOU CAN VIEW THE **gown worn by President Grover Cleveland's bride, FRANCES,** AT THE SMITHSONIAN'S NATIONAL MUSEUM OF AMERICAN HISTORY.

**4** The press was so intrigued by the CLEVELAND COUPLE that they used TELESCOPES to SPY on them during their honeymoon in Maryland.

**5** **Grover Cleveland** is the **only president** to have had his wedding **inside the White House.**

# 25 MATRIMONIAL FACTS ABOUT

**6** ALTHOUGH HE DIDN'T GET MARRIED IN THE WHITE HOUSE, PRESIDENT JOHN TYLER WAS THE **first president to tie the knot** WHILE IN OFFICE.

**7** Maria Monroe, the daughter of **President James Monroe,** was the first child of a president to be married in the White House, in 1820.

**8** MORE **White House weddings** HAVE TAKEN PLACE IN THE **Blue Room** THAN IN ANY OTHER ROOM IN THE HOME.

**9** First daughter **Nellie Grant,** then 19, **married a wealthy Englishman** in an elaborate White House wedding in 1874.

**10** JUST THE **LACE ON NELLIE'S WEDDING GOWN—** WHICH FEATURED A SIX-FOOT (1.8-M)-LONG TRAIN— **COST $1,500.**

**11** Nellie's father, President Ulysses S. Grant, was said to have disapproved of the union and cried throughout the ceremony.

**12** PRESIDENT **RUTHERFORD B. HAYES** HOSTED A WEDDING **FOR HIS NIECE** EMILY IN THE EAST ROOM OF THE WHITE HOUSE IN 1878.

**13** DURING THE CEREMONY, THE BRIDE AND GROOM STOOD UNDER A GIANT BELL CREATED BY THE WHITE HOUSE GARDENER FROM 15,000 ROSEBUDS.

**14** THOUSANDS OF PEOPLE PACKED THE STREETS surrounding the White House to catch a glimpse of PRESIDENT THEODORE ROOSEVELT'S DAUGHTER ALICE on her wedding day in 1906.

**15** AT THE WEDDING **RECEPTION,** ALICE FAMOUSLY **CUT THE CAKE** WITH A **SWORD.**

**16** TWO OF PRESIDENT WOODROW WILSON'S THREE DAUGHTERS MARRIED IN THE WHITE HOUSE; ONE IN 1913 AND THE OTHER IN 1914.

**17** FIVE OF ELEANOR AND FRANKLIN D. ROOSEVELT'S CHILDREN WERE MARRIED DURING THEIR 12-YEAR ADMINISTRATION, THOUGH NONE OF THEM CHOSE TO WED IN THE WHITE HOUSE.

**18** Luci Baines Johnson, Lyndon B. Johnson's daughter, wore a gown with a **nine-foot (2.7-m)-long train** in her White House wedding.

# WHITE HOUSE WEDDINGS

**19** FIFTY-FIVE MILLION PEOPLE TUNED INTO THEIR TVs TO WATCH LUCI'S WEDDING, WHICH WAS BROADCAST LIVE.

**20** In 1971, President RICHARD M. NIXON'S daughter TRICIA married lawyer EDWARD FINCH COX in the White House Rose Garden.

**21** The couple's **wedding cake,** made with **400 egg whites,** was a towering **seven feet** (2.1 m) **tall** and weighed **350 pounds** (159 kg).

**22** PRESIDENT George H. W. Bush's daughter, **DOROTHY, WED AT** Camp David in **1992—THE ONLY PRESIDENTIAL CHILD TO BE MARRIED AT THE RETREAT.**

**23** IN 1994, FIRST LADY **HILLARY CLINTON'S BROTHER,** ANTHONY RODHAM, **MARRIED** NICOLE BOXER IN THE **ROSE GARDEN.**

**24** After **first daughter Jenna Bush** wed in Texas, she and her husband, Henry Hager, were honored at a **White House reception.**

**25** Brides and grooms who send wedding invitations to the White House will receive in return a greeting from the PRESIDENT and first lady.

**1** VISITORS TO THE **BLUE ROOM** CAN SIT ON 200-YEAR-OLD **FRENCH FURNITURE** PURCHASED BY PRESIDENT JAMES MONROE.

**2** Some of the **BLUE SILK** upholstery of the Blue Room's furniture features **EAGLE** motifs.

**3** IN 1961, FIRST LADY JACQUELINE KENNEDY HAD A **French decorating firm** REDESIGN MOST OF THE ROOMS IN THE WHITE HOUSE USING **historic objects.**

**4** First Lady NELLIE TAFT decorated the White House with Asian artifacts she brought from her TRAVELS to the Philippines and Japan.

**5** White House residents can DECORATE THEIR BEDROOMS any way they want—down to the PAINT COLOR.

# 25 DESIGNER FACTS ABOUT

**6** When first daughter **CHELSEA CLINTON** lived in the White House, she **HUNG POSTERS** on her bedroom walls.

**7** FIRST DAUGHTER AMY CARTER SELECTED THE **VICTORIAN FURNITURE** FOR HER ROOM FROM THE WHITE HOUSE'S COLLECTION **OF HISTORIC OBJECTS.**

**8** Each incoming president receives money from **CONGRESS** to **REDECORATE** the rooms of the White House.

**9** Changes to the **State Dining Room** require the permission of a **special committee.**

**10** FIRST LADY NANCY REAGAN **USED ONE MILLION DOLLARS** IN DONATIONS FROM WEALTHY FRIENDS TO RENOVATE PARTS OF **THE WHITE HOUSE.**

**11** An artist created an **EXACT MODEL OF THE WHITE HOUSE,** built on a scale of one inch (2.5 cm) to one foot (30 cm).

**12** The model included every tiny detail, down to the **MINI WORKING TV SETS,** tiny **CRYSTAL CHANDELIERS,** paintings, and carpets.

**13** THE DIPLOMATIC RECEPTION ROOM FEATURES RARE, 183-YEAR-OLD WALLPAPER DEPICTING SCENES FROM EARLY AMERICA.

**14** The enormous 156-year-old **Lincoln bed**—now located in the Lincoln Bedroom—is almost **two feet (61 cm)** longer than a king-size bed.

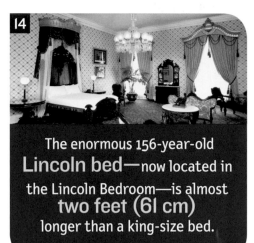

**15** Before leaving the White House, Jacqueline Kennedy put a PLAQUE IN THE LINCOLN BEDROOM memorializing her late husband, President John F. Kennedy.

**16** FIRST LADY MARY LINCOLN PURCHASED THE FAMOUS BED AND OTHER LUXURIES LIKE LACE CURTAINS AND SATIN-COVERED CHAIRS TO DECORATE ROOMS IN THE WHITE HOUSE.

**17** President John Tyler illuminated parts of the White House with **lamps fueled by lard oil** made from pork fat.

**18** The lamps FILLED THE HOUSE WITH A BAD SMELL which would drift to the upstairs bedrooms.

# WHITE HOUSE DECOR

**19** The GREEN ROOM originally got its name from a green canvas floorcloth laid by President THOMAS JEFFERSON.

**20** Later, President James Monroe—who played cards in the Green Room—added green **silk drapes and furniture** upholstered in the hue.

**21** There's a 108-YEAR-OLD MEDALLION of the United States seal on the CEILING OF THE OVAL OFFICE.

**22** THE MEDALLION— A BALD EAGLE CLUTCHING AN OLIVE BRANCH AND 13 ARROWS IN ITS TALONS—WAS IN THE ORIGINAL OVAL OFFICE, BUILT IN 1909.

**23** There are FOUR FIREPLACES in the EAST ROOM alone.

**24** First Lady MAMIE EISENHOWER decorated most of her private quarters of the White House in SHADES OF PINK.

**25** DURING THE EISENHOWERS' TIME IN THE WHITE HOUSE FROM 1953 TO 1961, A PAINT COMPANY RELEASED A SHADE IN "FIRST LADY PINK" NAMED AFTER MAMIE'S FAVORITE COLOR.

**1** To be president, you must be at least **35 years old**.

**2** YOU MUST ALSO BE A **NATURAL-BORN U.S. CITIZEN** AND HAVE LIVED IN THE COUNTRY FOR AT LEAST **14 YEARS**.

**3** The presidential family must **pay for all of the food they eat** in the White House, plus toilet paper and toothpaste.

**4** The first family also PAYS FOR ITS OWN DRY CLEANING— although staff members drop it off and PICK IT UP!

**5** At a White House party you **MUST STAND** when the president and first lady **ENTER THE ROOM.**

# 25 WHITE HOUSE

**6** Party guests are **EXPECTED TO STAY** as long as the **PRESIDENT DOES.**

**7** EACH PRESIDENT SETS HIS OR HER **OWN RULES ABOUT DRESS CODE** IN THE WHITE HOUSE.

**8** President George W. Bush required that men wear a coat and tie in the Oval Office at all times.

**9** President Barack Obama **LOOSENED UP THAT RULE** within his first week in office, tending to do the job **WITHOUT A SUIT JACKET ON.**

**10** Members of a college lacrosse team CAUSED A PANIC AFTER GREETING PRESIDENT GEORGE W. BUSH WHILE **wearing flip-flops**—WHICH HE HAD **banned** FROM THE WHITE HOUSE.

**11** When meeting in the Cabinet Room, **THE PRESIDENT ALWAYS SITS AT THE CENTER** of the table opposite the vice president.

THE PRESIDENT
JANUARY 20, 2009

**12** Other **Cabinet members** sit in **assigned chairs** depending on **ranking** and dates of service.

**13** The **presidential motorcade** is allowed to **run red lights** and **drive** above the speed limit.

**14** The motorcade is also given **right-of-way**, meaning other drivers are **expected to pull over** to let it pass by on the road.

**15** George Washington asked **PEOPLE TO CALL HIM MR. PRESIDENT** when they spoke to him.

**16** TODAY, WE STILL SAY **"Mr. President."**

**17** When a **woman is elected president,** she'll be called **Madam President.**

# RULES TO LIVE BY

**18** THE PRESIDENTIAL SEAL APPEARS ON ALL CORRESPONDENCE FROM THE PRESIDENT AS WELL AS ON OFFICIAL INVITATIONS FROM THE WHITE HOUSE.

**19** On **INAUGURATION DAY,** it's protocol for the incoming president to arrive at the North Portico and be **MET BY THE OUTGOING PRESIDENT.**

**20** THE TWO THEN **travel together from the White House to the Capitol** FOR THE SWEARING-IN CEREMONY.

**21** The president orders when a flag should be flown at half-staff outside of the White House—and throughout the country.

**22** Typically, flags are flown half-staff when prominent **GOVERNMENT OFFICIALS DIE,** and after **MAJOR NATIONAL TRAGEDIES.**

**23** For more than **40 years, people on public tours** of the White House were **banned from taking photos inside.**

**24** In 2015, the ban was lifted and now **YOU CAN TAKE PHOTOS THROUGHOUT THE WHITE HOUSE.**

**25** LEAVE YOUR VIDEO CAMERAS, TABLETS, AND SELFIE STICKS AT HOME—THEY'RE ALL STILL A NO-NO ON WHITE HOUSE TOURS.

# 15 COOL FACTS ABOUT

**1** Each president is catered to by a **full-time staff**, including chefs, a social secretary, a chief calligrapher, groundskeepers, and butlers.

**2** On the ground floor of the White House are such **shops** as a **carpenter's**, an **engineer's**, a **chocolatier's**, and a **florist's**.

**3** The chief floral designer is one of the permanent staff positions in the White House.

**4** Deliveries of fresh flowers arrive at the White House almost daily.

**5** First Lady Lucy Hayes hired the first **full-time** floral arrangers—known as **bouquet makers**—in the late 1870s.

**6** White House carpenters **make and repair** furniture and equipment in the carpenters' shop and engineers' shop.

**7** The president will **never mow the lawn: The grounds superintendent** oversees the grounds around the White House.

**8** The grounds superintendent has also looked after **presidents' dogs.**

Every day there is something going on at the White House: A band performs on the South Lawn to celebrate the Fourth of July.

Barack Obama's dog Bo

# EVERYDAY LIFE AT THE WHITE HOUSE

**9** The White House **doctor's office** is equipped with two examination rooms used by the president and staff.

**10** The doctor also travels as part of the presidential entourage on the campaign trail and on trips.

**11** The president's plane, **Air Force One**, is staffed by a doctor and contains a **pharmacy** and an **operating table**.

**12** Aside from the White House, there is a **dental clinic** at the presidential retreat at **Camp David**.

**13** The White House pastry chefs use the **pastry shop** to work on decorative desserts, like candy **centerpieces** and pulled **sugar flowers**.

**14** The **humidity** levels in the **chocolate shop** are carefully controlled so that the **delicate desserts** can hold their shape.

**15** A team of **housekeepers** is always on hand to **make beds**, vacuum, and **pick up after** the president and family.

# KEY WORDS

**address** a formal speech delivered to an audience

**administration** the group of people who manage, make rules for, and run an organization

**Air Force One** generally, any U.S. Air Force plane with the U.S. president on board but mostly the planes specifically designed and used for the commander in chief of the armed forces, the president

**ambassador** an appointed official who represents his or her country's government while living in a foreign country

**artifact** any human-made object or item that usually has cultural or historical importance

**assassination** the act of murdering by sudden or secret attack often for political reasons; usually refers to a prominent person, such as the president

**bill** a law that has been proposed to Congress, but has not yet been passed; a bill becomes a law if the president signs it; a president may also veto the bill

**briefing** giving precise, important, or essential information

**bust** a sculpture of a human that includes only the head and neck and typically part of the shoulders and chest

**Cabinet** the group of people who advise the president; includes the vice president and the heads of the executive departments

**commander in chief** the title given to the president as the civilian leader of the U.S. armed forces

**Congress** the legislative branch of the U.S. government, which includes the Senate and the House of Representatives

**constitution** a document that is the highest law in the land and defines the federal government; the United States Constitution includes seven articles and 27 amendments

**curator** the person responsible for studying and preserving valuable items in a collection, as in a museum, art gallery, or the White House

**decor** the style and layout of the inside of a building, including paintwork, wallpaper, curtains, carpets, and furniture

**Democratic Party** one of the two major contemporary political parties in the United States; *see also* Republican Party

**dignitary** a person of importance or honor such as a head of state, monarch, or senator

**diplomatic** related to an appointed official—diplomat— who represents his or her country's government when visiting a foreign country; *see also* ambassador

**East Wing** the White House addition containing the social office, the visitors' entrance, and the office of the first lady

**economy** work and finance of a city, region, or country related to producing, selling, and exchanging goods and services

**election** a formal and organized process of choosing someone to hold public office, such as the presidency, by voting

**Emancipation Proclamation** a declaration made by President Abraham Lincoln in 1863 that all slaves in parts of the country not yet in the Union of the United States (the Confederacy) were to be free forever

**executive** the branch of government headed by the president; it includes the president, vice president, and 15 main executive departments

**Executive Mansion** the original name of the White House before it was given that title in 1901

**federal** related to the whole country; also an architectural style

**first lady** the formal name given to the president's wife or official hostess

**government** the group of people in charge of a country, state, or area

**head of state** the person who holds the highest position in a national government, such as a president, king, or queen

**House of Representatives** the part of government made up of elected representatives of each state

**Inauguration** the ceremony formally introducing the president into office

**lay in state** to place the dead body of an important person in a government building so the public can pay their respects

**limousine** a large, luxurious, often chauffeur-driven car

**Marine One** any helicopter used as an Air Force One plane

**matrimonial** anything related to marriage

**mess** a U.S. military term for cafeteria or place to socialize

**military** the armed forces—the army, navy, and air force

**monarch** a sovereign head of state, such as a king, queen, or emperor

**oath of office** a declaration the president must make before undertaking the duties of the office; includes the promise to preserve, protect, and defend the U.S. Constitution

**office** a position or job in government; also a room in which someone works

**Oval Office** the official office of the president, named for its oval shape

**political party** a group of people with similar beliefs on governing a country that try to get candidates elected to represent them

**portico** a row of columns supporting a roof typically found at the entrance of a building; the White House has a South Portico and a North Portico

**President's House** the name briefly used to describe the Executive Mansion before it was built

**President's Park** the official name of the White House Grounds and the surrounding parkland

**press secretary** the chief spokesperson for the president of the United States; appointed by the president, but not a member of the Cabinet, he or she gives regular briefings and interviews to news outlets at the White House

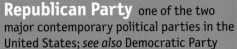

**Republican Party** one of the two major contemporary political parties in the United States; *see also* Democratic Party

**resignation** the act of officially stepping down from a position, such as the presidency

**Secret Service** the law enforcement agency responsible for providing protection to the president and investigating certain types of financial crime

**Senate** a group of elected officials that makes up half of the legislative branch of government; there are two senators per state for a total of 100 senators

**Situation Room** a complex of rooms in the White House that is staffed 24 hours a day, seven days a week to monitor national and world intelligence information

**state** one of the parts of a nation; in the United States each of the 50 states has its own government and laws

**state dinner** a formal, lavish White House affair honoring a visiting head of government or reigning monarch

**Supreme Court** the highest court in the land, headed by the Chief Justice

**swearing in** an official ceremony where the president takes an oath of office; occurs during the Inauguration

**tenure** holding a position or term of office in an organization

**term** the time that a politician may hold office; for example, according to the U.S. Constitution, a person can serve as president of the United States for no more than two four-year terms

**veto** the power of the president to reject a bill

**West Wing** the White House addition housing presidential office space including the Oval Office, the Cabinet Room, the Situation Room, the Roosevelt Room, the Press Briefing Room, and offices for the president's closest aides

**White House** the home and office of the president of the United States

# DATES IN WHITE

HISTORY HAS BEEN MADE IN THE WHITE HOUSE EVER SINCE THE CORNERSTONE WAS LAID IN 1792. BUT THE BUILDING HAS ITS OWN HISTORY, TOO! CHECK OUT THESE HISTORIC WHITE HOUSE DATES AND TAKE A PEEK INSIDE THE BUILDING THE PRESIDENT CALLS HOME.

**1790** The U.S. Congress votes to build and furnish a house and office for the president in the newly created capital city of Washington, D.C.

**1792** The cornerstone of the White House is laid.

**1800** President John Adams and his wife, Abigail, move into the brand-new—and partially completed—White House.

**1805** Thomas Jefferson holds the first Inaugural open house and later opens the White House doors for public tours and receptions on New Year's Day and the Fourth of July.

**1814** British troops seize control of Washington and set the White House on fire.

**1817** President James Monroe moves into the reconstructed White House—rebuilt from the fire according to plans by James Hoban, the original White House architect.

**1833** Running water is installed in the White House.

**1863** President Abraham Lincoln effectively ends slavery after signing the Emancipation Proclamation on January 1 in his White House study.

**1871** President Ulysses S. Grant and his wife host the first ever state dinner, welcoming King David Kalākaua of the Sandwich Islands, modern-day Hawaii.

**1879** The first telephone is installed in the White House.

**1891** The White House is wired for electricity.

**1902** President Theodore Roosevelt begins a major renovation of the White House, adding an executive office building later called the West Wing.

# HOUSE HISTORY

**1909** The West Wing is doubled in size and the Oval Office is built.

**1927** A third floor is added to the White House.

**1929** A Christmas Eve fire in 1929 guts the White House's West Wing.

**1934** The East Wing is constructed, including three stories of offices, a bomb shelter, and a movie theater.

**1942** Camp David, located about an hour away from the White House, is built as a weekend retreat for the president.

**1945** President Harry S. Truman announces the end of World War II from the Oval Office.

**1952** A massive renovation of the White House is completed after four years of construction.

**1963** President John F. Kennedy is assassinated while visiting Dallas, Texas. President Lyndon B. Johnson is sworn into office on an airplane.

**1964** The Civil Rights Act is signed by President Johnson and witnessed by Martin Luther King, Jr., in the East Room.

**1974** President Richard M. Nixon makes history as the first president in history to resign from office.

**1981** President Ronald Reagan appoints the first woman to the Supreme Court, Sandra Day O'Connor, in a Rose Garden ceremony.

**1992** The Internet makes its debut in the White House, and President George H. W. Bush sends the first email as a president in office.

**2000** The White House celebrates the 200th anniversary of its first occupancy.

**2008** Barack Obama is elected as the first African-American president in U.S. history.

**2016** Famous businessman and reality TV show star Donald J. Trump is elected as the 45th president of the United States.

# PRESIDENTS

Forty-four people have served as president of the United States. Several have served more than one term in office. Grover Cleveland served two non-consecutive terms in office, being the nation's 22nd and 24th president. Franklin D. Roosevelt served the longest, with four terms and more than 12 years.

**1** **Name:** George Washington
**Nickname:** Father of His Country
**Term of office:** April 1789 to March 1797
**Political party:** Federalist
**First lady:** Martha Washington, wife

**2** **Name:** John Adams
**Nickname:** Father of American Independence
**Term of office:** March 1797 to March 1801
**Political party:** Federalist
**First lady:** Abigail Adams, wife

**3** **Name:** Thomas Jefferson
**Nickname:** Father of the Declaration of Independence
**Term of office:** March 1801 to March 1809
**Political party:** Democratic Republican
**First lady:** Martha Jefferson Randolph, daughter

**4** **Name:** James Madison
**Nickname:** Father of the Constitution
**Term of office:** March 1809 to March 1817
**Political party:** Democratic Republican
**First lady:** Dolley Madison, wife

**5** **Name:** James Monroe
**Nickname:** Era of Good Feelings President
**Term of office:** March 1817 to March 1825
**Political party:** Democratic Republican
**First lady:** Elizabeth Monroe, wife

**6** **Name:** John Quincy Adams
**Nickname:** Old Man Eloquent
**Term of office:** March 1825 to March 1829
**Political party:** Democratic Republican
**First lady:** Louisa Adams, wife

**7** **Name:** Andrew Jackson
**Nickname:** Old Hickory
**Term of office:** March 1829 to March 1837
**Political party:** Democrat
**First lady:** Emily Donelson, niece

**8** **Name:** Martin Van Buren
**Nickname:** Little Magician
**Term of office:** March 1837 to March 1841
**Political party:** Democrat
**First lady:** Angelica Van Buren, daughter-in-law

**9** **Name:** William Henry Harrison
**Nickname:** Tippecanoe
**Term of office:** March 1841 to April 1841
**Political party:** Whig
**First lady:** Jane Harrison, daughter-in-law

**10** **Name:** John Tyler
**Nickname:** His Accidency
**Term of office:** April 1841 to March 1845
**Political party:** Whig
**First ladies:** Letitia Tyler, first wife; Priscilla Tyler, daughter-in-law; Letitia Tyler Semple, daughter; Julia Tyler, second wife

**11** **Name:** James K. Polk
**Nickname:** Young Hickory
**Term of office:** March 1845 to March 1849
**Political party:** Democrat
**First lady:** Sarah Polk, wife

**12** **Name:** Zachary Taylor
**Nickname:** Old Rough-and-Ready
**Term of office:** March 1849 to July 1850
**Political party:** Whig
**First ladies:** Margaret Taylor, wife; Mary Elizabeth Taylor Bliss, daughter

**13** **Name:** Millard Fillmore
**Nickname:** Last of the Whigs
**Term of office:** July 1850 to March 1853
**Political party:** Whig
**First ladies:** Abigail Fillmore, wife; Mary Abigail Fillmore, daughter

**14** **Name:** Franklin Pierce
**Nickname:** Handsome Frank
**Term of office:** March 1853 to March 1857
**Political party:** Democrat
**First lady:** Jane Pierce, wife

**15** **Name:** James Buchanan
**Nickname:** Ten-Cent Jimmy
**Term of office:** March 1857 to March 1861
**Political party:** Democrat
**First lady:** Harriet Lane, niece

**16** **Name:** Abraham Lincoln
**Nickname:** Honest Abe
**Term of office:** March 1861 to April 1865
**Political party:** Republican (formerly Whig)
**First lady:** Mary Lincoln, wife

**17** **Name:** Andrew Johnson
**Nickname:** The Veto President
**Term of office:** April 1865 to March 1869
**Political party:** Democrat
**First ladies:** Eliza Johnson, wife; Martha Johnson Patterson, daughter

**18** **Name:** Ulysses S. Grant
**Nickname:** Unconditional Surrender Grant
**Term of office:** March 1869 to March 1877
**Political party:** Republican
**First lady:** Julia Grant, wife

**19** **Name:** Rutherford B. Hayes
**Nickname:** His Fraudulency
**Term of office:** March 1877 to March 1881
**Political party:** Republican
**First lady:** Lucy Hayes, wife

**20** **Name:** James A. Garfield
**Nickname:** Preacher President
**Term of office:** March 1881 to September 1881
**Political party:** Republican
**First lady:** Lucretia Garfield, wife

**21** **Name:** Chester A. Arthur
**Nickname:** Elegant Arthur
**Term of office:** September 1881 to March 1885
**Political party:** Republican
**First lady:** Mary "Molly" McElroy, sister

**22 & 24** **Name:** Grover Cleveland
**Nickname:** Uncle Jumbo
**Term of office:** first administration: March 1885 to March 1889; second administration: March 1893 to March 1897
**Political party:** Democrat
**First ladies:** Rose Cleveland, sister; Frances Cleveland, wife

**23** **Name:** Benjamin Harrison
**Nickname:** Little Ben
**Term of office:** March 1889 to March 1893
**Political party:** Republican
**First ladies:** Caroline Harrison, wife; Mary Harrison McKee, daughter

**25** **Name:** William McKinley
**Nickname:** Idol of Ohio
**Term of office:** March 1897 to September 1901
**Political party:** Republican
**First lady:** Ida McKinley, wife

**26** **Name:** Theodore Roosevelt
**Nickname:** Teddy
**Term of office:** September 1901 to March 1909
**Political party:** Republican
**First lady:** Edith Roosevelt, second wife

**27** **Name:** William Howard Taft
**Nickname:** Big Bill
**Term of office:** March 1909 to March 1913
**Political party:** Republican
**First lady:** Helen "Nellie" Taft, wife

**28** **Name:** Woodrow Wilson
**Nickname:** Professor
**Term of office:** March 1913 to March 1921
**Political party:** Democrat
**First ladies:** Ellen Wilson, first wife; Margaret Wilson, daughter; Edith Wilson, second wife

**29** **Name:** Warren G. Harding
**Nickname:** Wobbly Warren
**Term of office:** March 1921 to August 1923
**Political party:** Republican
**First lady:** Florence Harding, wife

**30** **Name:** Calvin Coolidge
**Nickname:** Silent Cal
**Term of office:** August 1923 to March 1929
**Political party:** Republican
**First lady:** Grace Coolidge, wife

**31** **Name:** Herbert Hoover
**Nickname:** Chief
**Term of office:** March 1929 to March 1933
**Political party:** Republican
**First lady:** Lou Hoover, wife

**32** **Name:** Franklin D. Roosevelt
**Nickname:** FDR
**Term of office:** March 1933 to April 1945
**Political party:** Democrat
**First lady:** Eleanor Roosevelt, wife

**33** **Name:** Harry S. Truman
**Nickname:** Give 'Em Hell Harry
**Term of office:** April 1945 to January 1953
**Political party:** Democrat
**First lady:** Bess Truman, wife

**34** **Name:** Dwight D. Eisenhower
**Nickname:** Ike
**Term of office:** January 1953 to January 1961
**Political party:** Republican
**First lady:** Mamie Eisenhower, wife

**35** **Name:** John F. Kennedy
**Nickname:** JFK
**Term of office:** January 1961 to November 1963
**Political party:** Democrat
**First lady:** Jacqueline Kennedy, wife

**36** **Name:** Lyndon B. Johnson
**Nickname:** LBJ
**Term of office:** November 1963 to January 1969
**Political party:** Democrat
**First lady:** Claudia Alta "Lady Bird" Johnson, wife

**37** **Name:** Richard M. Nixon
**Nickname:** Tricky Dick
**Term of office:** January 1969 to August 1974
**Political party:** Republican
**First lady:** Pat Nixon, wife

**38** **Name:** Gerald R. Ford
**Nickname:** Jerry
**Term of office:** August 1974 to January 1977
**Political party:** Republican
**First lady:** Elizabeth "Betty" Ford, wife

**39** **Name:** James Carter
**Nickname:** Jimmy
**Term of office:** January 1977 to January 1981
**Political party:** Democrat
**First lady:** Rosalynn Carter, wife

**40** **Name:** Ronald Reagan
**Nickname:** Dutch
**Term of office:** January 1981 to January 1989
**Political party:** Republican
**First lady:** Nancy Reagan, wife

**41** **Name:** George H. W. Bush
**Nickname:** Poppy
**Term of office:** January 1989 to January 1993
**Political party:** Republican
**First lady:** Barbara Bush, wife

**42** **Name:** Bill Clinton
**Nickname:** Comeback Kid
**Term of office:** January 1993 to January 2001
**Political party:** Democrat
**First lady:** Hillary Clinton, wife

**43** **Name:** George W. Bush
**Nickname:** Dubya (W.)
**Term of office:** January 2001 to January 2009
**Political party:** Republican
**First lady:** Laura Bush, wife

**44** **Name:** Barack Obama
**Nickname:** Barry
**Term of office:** January 2009 to January 2017
**Political party:** Democrat
**First lady:** Michelle Obama, wife

**45** **Name:** Donald J. Trump
**Nickname:** The Donald
**Term of office:** January 2017 to
**Political party:** Republican
**First lady:** Melania Trump, wife

# INDEX

# RESOURCES

To learn more about the White House, the U.S. presidents, and Washington, D.C., look into these sources:

## BOOKS

**Bausum, Ann.** *Our Country's Presidents*. National Geographic, 2017.

**Grove, Noel.** *Inside the White House.* National Geographic, 2013.

**Kostyal, Karen.** *George Washington's Rules to Live By.* National Geographic, 2013.

**Monkman, Betty C.** *The White House: Its Historic Furnishings and First Families.* Abbeville Press, 2014.

**Panchyk, Richard.** *Washington, D.C., History for Kids.* Chicago Review Press, 2016.

**Pickens, Jennifer.** *Pets at the White House: 50 Years of Presidents and Their Pets.* Fife and Drum Press, 2012.

**Trounstine, Connie.** *Fingerprints on the Table: The Story of the White House Treaty Table.* White House Historical Association, 2013.

**White House Historical Association.** *The White House: An Historic Guide.* White House Historical Association, 2012.

## WEBSITES

www.firstladies.org
www.millercenter.org/president
www.presidentialpetmuseum.com
www.washington.org
www.whitehouse.gov
www.whitehousehistory.org
www.whitehousemuseum.org

# CREDITS

Copyright © 2017 National Geographic Partners, LLC

Published by National Geographic Partners, LLC. All rights reserved. Reproduction of the whole or any part of the contents without written permission from the publisher is prohibited.

PRODUCED FOR NATIONAL GEOGRAPHIC PARTNERS BY BENDER RICHARDSON WHITE

Since 1888, the National Geographic Society has funded more than 12,000 research, exploration, and preservation projects around the world. The Society receives funds from National Geographic Partners, LLC, funded in part by your purchase. A portion of the proceeds from this book supports this vital work. To learn more, visit natgeo.com/info.

NATIONAL GEOGRAPHIC and Yellow Border Design are trademarks of the National Geographic Society, used under license.

For more information, please visit nationalgeographic .com, call 1-800-647-5463, or write to the following address:

National Geographic Partners
1145 17th Street N.W.
Washington, D.C. 20036-4688 U.S.A.

Visit us online at nationalgeographic.com/books

For librarians and teachers: ngchildrensbooks.org

More for kids from National Geographic:
kids.nationalgeographic.com

For information about special discounts for bulk purchases, please contact National Geographic Books Special Sales: specialsales@natgeo.com

For rights or permissions inquiries, please contact National Geographic Books Subsidiary Rights: bookrights@natgeo.com

Designed by Malcolm Smythe
Cover designed by Julide Dengel

Hardcover ISBN: 978-1-4263-2873-2
Reinforced library binding ISBN: 978-1-4263-2874-9

The publisher would like to thank Marcia Anderson, vice president of publishing and executive editor at the White House Historical Association, and the project team of Bender Richardson White: Lionel Bender, Editor/Project Manager; Sarah Wassner Flynn, Author; Catherine Farley, Copy Editor/Proofreader; Ben White, Art Director; Sharon Dortenzio, Picture Editor; Malcolm Smythe, Designer; Kim Richardson, Production Manager; Amanda Rock, Fact Checker; and Amron Gravett, Indexer.

Printed in China
17/RRDS/1